Twayne's United States Authors Series

EDITOR OF THIS VOLUME

Warren French

Indiana University

René Wellek

TUSAS 410

René Wellek

RENÉ WELLEK

By MARTIN BUCCO
Colorado State University

TWAYNE PUBLISHERS

A DIVISION OF G. K. HALL & CO., BOSTON

Published in 1981 by Twayne Publishers,
A Division of G. K. Hall & Co.
All Rights Reserved

Printed on permanent/durable acid-free paper and bound
in the United States of America

First Printing

Library of Congress Cataloging in Publication Data

Bucco, Martin.
René Wellek.

(Twayne's United States authors series; TUSAS 410)
Bibliography: p. 168–73
Includes index.
1. Wellek, René.
PN75.W4B8   809   80–25823
ISBN 0–8057–7339–8

For Mario and Ann—
Dolores, Anita, and Ron

Contents

About the Author

A professor of American literature and literary criticism at Colorado State University, Martin Bucco was born in Newark, New Jersey, in 1929. He attended public schools in Essex County, New Jersey, and earned his B.A. at New Mexico Highlands University, his M.A. at Columbia University, and his Ph.D. at the University of Missouri. Recognized many times for his excellence in the classroom, Martin Bucco began his teaching career in New Mexico and North Dakota. He has been a visiting professor at Northern Arizona University and the University of the Pacific, and he has traveled and lectured in Europe. Besides writing many scholarly reviews, he has published essays on such figures as Sherwood Anderson, Thomas Bulfinch, Truman Capote, Theodore Dreiser, Ralph Ellison, Sinclair Lewis, and Mark Twain. Professor Bucco's first book in TUSAS, *Wilbur Daniel Steele*, appeared in 1972. He points out that he first read a story by Steele and first heard of René Wellek in 1949, in Emerson R. Marks's Freshman English class at Newark Rutgers. Martin Bucco's other books are *The Voluntary Tongue* (1957), "Introduction," *The Age of Fable* (1966), *Frank Waters* (1969), *An American Tragedy Notes* (1974), and *E. W. Howe* (1977). The author has received a number of literary prizes and awards, including grants from the National Foundation on the Arts and the Humanities. In 1977, he participated in the Summer Seminar in Contemporary Literary Criticism at Yale University. In 1982, Martin Bucco will assume the office of president of the Western Literature Association.

Preface

This book is the first full-length introduction to René Wellek. In our time, this contemporary American writer is in the world of Western letters what the Englishman George Saintsbury was in his: the most influential academic critic and critical historian. Further, René Wellek is an important literary theorist. His books, essays, and reviews are brilliant integrations of theory, history, and criticism. They also reveal a firm grasp of the history of ideas. Immune neither to controversy nor to adverse criticism, his work has long attracted scholars, students, and educated readers of literature and literary studies.

Now in twenty-two translations, *Theory of Literature* has joined such classics as John Livingston Lowes's *Road to Xanadu*, C. S. Lewis's *Allegory of Love*, and Erich Auerbach's *Mimesis*. (But even champions of "Wellek and Warren," as *Theory of Literature* is familiarly known, frequently confuse René Wellek's friend and collaborator Austin Warren—such are the vagaries of life—with his friend and colleague Robert Penn Warren.) To many critical readers, René Wellek's many essays on critical concepts are "indispensable." His one-man, multi-volume *History of Modern Criticism: 1750–1950*, though unfinished, is already a "monument" to humane scholarship. "Even in an age of great scholars," Mark Schorer once commented, "such a man is not commonly come by."

Accordingly, a number of the finest universities and academies in America and in Europe have honored him, as indeed have fellow editors and critics. Alfred Owen Aldridge, for example, has acknowledged René Wellek in the *Times Literary Supplement* as "the most eminent and learned exponent of comparative literature in the world." Joseph P. Strelka has judged him in the *Yearbook of Comparative Criticism* as "the most universal and greatest literary critic of our time." And *Svenska Dageblat* has suggested in its section *Läst och hört* that the Nobel Prize for Literary History—were there such a Nobel Prize!—should go to Wellek. Understandably, Laurence Lerner has owned up in the *Review of English Studies:* "No one is qualified to review René Wellek."

Knowing as "small German and less Czech" as Professor Lerner, I harbor no illusions about my own ability to review René Wellek. Still, as a teacher of literature and criticism I have managed over the years to infect both graduates and undergraduates with something like my own fascination with Wellek's critical personality—his awesome breadth of reading, his depth of reasoning, the centrality— the sanity—of his literary and critical views. This study, then, is in a real sense a considered extension of my classroom enthusiasm.

My primary aim is to present to divers readers a unitary view of René Wellek—a description of his ideas, his development, his books. In reflecting his major work and its reception, I touch, to be sure, on some of his scattered essays and many reviews. In my exposition, too, his "voice" is always near and clear. Again, since there is no full biography, I have assembled as Chapter 1 a sketch of his life in Europe and America. In the second chapter, I discuss Wellek's lesser-known early writings in English and Czech. Chapter 3 is devoted to the influential *Theory of Literature*. In Chapter 4, I deal with the later writings, mostly the collected essays from mid-century to the present. The next two chapters should assist especially those who complain about inadequate summaries of the monumental *History of Modern Criticism:* Chapter 5 treats *The Later Eighteenth Century* and *The Romantic Age;* Chapter 6, *The Age of Transition* and *The Later Nineteenth Century*—and includes some indications of the shape of the two final volumes to come: twentieth-century Anglo-American and Continental criticism. Chapter 7 assesses René Wellek's influence and significance.

Of course, no overview can do justice to René Wellek's rich critical configurations. He himself once remarked: "Critics—like poems— cannot be paraphrased." Still, I trust that my bold outlines, if accurate, heighten René Wellek's critical intelligence, historical imagination, astonishing erudition, linguistic competence, and professional intrepidity. Also, I am all too aware that judgment of any writer— literary or critical—is not really possible until all writings are in. Again, one finds René Wellek salutary: "For practical purposes we need not postpone understanding to a distant future." In this unpostponed introduction, then, I presume, at least, that the tone is positive, the light steady, the account readable.

A grant from the National Endowment for the Humanities enabled me to enjoy the resources of Yale University for a summer. The librarians at Colorado State University have been especially helpful. For permission to quote from *Theory of Literature* by René Wellek and Austin Warren and from *A History of Modern Criticism: 1750–1950* by René Wellek, I thank Harcourt Brace Jovanovitch, Inc. and Yale University Press respectively. For various kindnesses, I take pleasure in acknowledging my indebtedness to Joseph W. Angell, Arthur Berndtson, Willard O. Eddy, Warren French, Geoffrey H. Hartman, Emerson R. Marks, John Clark Pratt, Kenneth Rock, Frank Vattano, and Nonna D. Wellek. Most of all, warm thanks go to René Wellek and to my wife, Edith Erickson Bucco.

MARTIN BUCCO

Colorado State University

Chronology

1903   René Wellek born August 22 in Vienna to Bronislav and Gabriele (von Zelewsky) Wellek.
1918   Moves with family to Prague.
1922   Enters Charles University, Prague.
1926   Receives Phil. D.
1927-   Postgraduate work, Princeton University.
1928
1928-   Instructor in German, Smith College.
1929
1929-   Instructor in German, Princeton University.
1930
1931–   *Privatdozent,* Charles University.
1935
1931   *Immanuel Kant in England: 1793–1838.*
1932   Marries Olga Brodská.
1935–   Lecturer, School of Slavonic Studies, University of London.
1939
1939   Emigrates to the United States. Lecturer, University of Iowa.
1941   *The Rise of English Literary History.* Associate Professor, Iowa. Editorial board, *Philological Quarterly* (1941–46).
1942   Fellow, Huntington Library.
1943   Son, Ivan Alexander, born.
1944   Professor of English, Iowa.
1946   Honorary M.A., Yale. Naturalized citizen of the United States. Professor of Slavic and Comparative Literature, Yale. Editorial board (1946–50), Modern Language Association.
1947   Visiting Summer Professor, University of Minnesota.
1948   Visiting Summer Professor, Columbia University. Chairman, Slavic Department, Yale.
1949   *Theory of Literature* (with Austin Warren). Editorial board, *Comparative Literature.* Fellow, Kenyon School. Com-

mittee on Research Activities (1949–55), Modern Language Association.

1950   Fellow, Silliman College, Yale. Visiting Professor, Harvard University. Lecturer, Princeton Seminars in Criticism. Fellow (1950–72), Indiana School of Letters.

1951–   Guggenheim Fellow.
1952

1952   Sterling Professor of Comparative Literature, Yale.

1953–   Visiting Professor, Harvard. Editorial board, Modern Language Association.
1954

1955   *A History of Modern Criticism* (Vols. I and II).

1956–   Guggenheim Fellow.
1957

1958   L.H.D., Lawrence College.

1959   Distinguished Service Award, American Council of Learned Societies.

1959–   Executive Council, Modern Language Association. Fulbright Research Scholar, Italy.
1960

1960   Chairman, Department of Comparative Literature, Yale. Litt.D., Harvard. Litt.D., Oxford University.

1961   President (1961–64), International Comparative Literature Association. Litt.D., University of Rome. Visiting Summer Professor, University of Hawaii.

1962   President (1962–66), Czechoslovakia Society of Arts and Sciences in America, Inc. President (1962–65), American Comparative Literature Association.

1963   *Essays on Czech Literature.* Visiting Summer Professor, University of California, Berkeley. *Concepts of Criticism.*

1964   Vice President, Modern Language Association. Litt.D., University of Maryland.

1965   *Confrontations. A History of Modern Criticism* (Vols. III and IV). Litt.D., Boston College.

1966–   Guggenheim Fellow.
1967

1967   Olga Wellek dies.

1968   Litt.D., Columbia University. Marries Nonna Dolodarenko Shaw.

1969   Fulbright Distinguished Lecturer, Germany.

1970   Litt.D., University of Montreal. Litt.D., University of Louvain. *Discriminations.*

1972	Litt.D., University of Michigan. Litt.D., University of Munich. Sterling Professor Emeritus, Yale.
1972–1973	Senior Fellow, National Endowment for the Humanities.
1973	Visiting Professor, Princeton University.
1974	President, Modern Humanities Research Association. Patton Professor of Comparative Literature, Indiana University.
1975	Litt.D., University of East Anglia.
1977	Senior Fellow, Society for the Humanities, Cornell University.
1979	Visiting Professor, University of California, San Diego. *Verdienstkreuz 1. Klasse für Kunst und Wissenschaft*, Innsbruck Congress, International Comparative Literature Association. Walker-Ames Professor, University of Washington.

CHAPTER 1

Europe and America

IN the fall of 1978, the distinguished American literary theorist, critical historian, and comparatist scholar René Wellek spoke at the Sterling Memorial Library, Yale University, on the occasion of an exhibition of his publications for the celebration of his seventy-fifth birthday. After outlining the main tasks ahead of him, the Sterling Professor Emeritus of Comparative Literature looked back on his writing life over the past fifty-four years and noted that his books reflected the many changes in literary scholarship and criticism. Still, he hoped that he had preserved his own integrity and a core of convictions. Wellek, whose impulse has always been to help clarify the methodological Tower of Babel, once explained: "My views and aspirations are best expounded in my books."[1] Many literary scholars the world over know the convictions and aspirations in Wellek's books, if not in all of his hundreds of scattered essays and reviews. Appealing also to the student of literature and criticism are the stages of René Wellek's remarkable development, particularly his formative years in Europe and the years preceding his acquiring American citizenship in 1946.

I Vienna

René Wellek was born in Vienna on August 22, 1903, the oldest of three children. In this old Hapsburg capital—cradle of much contemporary thought in psychology, medicine, philosophy, politics, art, music, and literature—Wellek and his younger brother, Albert (1904–1972), spent their boyhoods. The culture of Wellek's parents influenced his development profoundly. His father, Bronislav Wellek (1872–1959), then a government lawyer, was a Czech from a petty-bourgeois Catholic family in Prague. Known as a *Liedersänger*, a Wagnerian, and an opera reviewer, Bronislav Wellek

also was an ardent Czech nationalist and a biographer of the com-
poser Bedřich Smetana and a translator of the poets Jaroslav
Vrchlicky and J. S. Machar. René Wellek's mother, *née* Gabriele
von Zelewsky (1881–1950), came from a different background. Born
in Rome, she bloomed into a beauty who spoke German, Italian,
French, and English. René Wellek's maternal grandfather was a
West Prussian nobleman of Polish origin; Wellek's grandmother was
a Swiss Protestant from picturesque Schaffhausen. After the nobleman's death, his widow, son, and daughter traveled on the Continent. In Vienna, Gabriele von Zelewsky met Bronislav Wellek.

In the crowded capital the young couple and their sons moved
from apartment to apartment. From 1906 to 1908 Bronislav Wellek
served under the Austrian prime minister, Baron von Beck, to whom
he gave Czech lessons. In 1912 the Welleks settled in a large house
with garden and terrace. At home and in the kaleidoscopic Danubian
metropolis, René and Albert grew up in an atmosphere rich in
linguistic, aesthetic, political, and religious overtones. Since the
Protestantism of their Swiss grandmother prevailed in the family,
the Brothers Wellek had been baptized in the Lutheran Church.
Even the agnostic Bronislav became a nominal Lutheran.

As a boy René Wellek read voraciously. He and his brother developed "crazes" for all kinds of encyclopedic and historical information—geography, science, religion, literature, military campaigns.
Familiar with Viennese opera, René Wellek also took piano lessons.
At school he and his brother spoke German, but often encountered
anti-Czech feeling. At home and on vacations in the river valleys
and pinewoods of Bohemia, the brothers spoke Czech. A month
after he became ten, René Wellek started Latin lessons, and for
eight hours a week for eight years he read much of Livy, Cornelius
Nepos, Caesar, Cicero, Ovid, Vergil, Horace, Catullus, and Tacitus.[2]

During the First World War, René Wellek recalls, food in Vienna
grew scarce and cannon boomed in the Carpathians. When he was
thirteen he started Greek, and during the next three years he read
Xenophon, much Homer, some Plato and Lucian. During his con-
valescence from scarlet fever, his father read to him the whole of
The Pickwick Papers in German. When he returned finally to the
Währing *Gymnasium*, he was permitted to substitute English or
French for his interrupted Greek studies. Wellek's choice of English
influenced his life decisively. Though he still spent long hours at
his Latin, he grew increasingly sceptical of mechanical instruction.

II *Prague*

With the collapse of the Austro-Hungarian. Empire in 1918, the
Welleks (and infant Elizabeth) moved to the ancient cathedral city
of Prague, that picturesque settlement at the entrance to Eastern
Europe. "Czechoslovakia after the war," Wellek notes, "more than
ever, stood at the crossroads of all cultural influences, in consequence of her geographical position, her Slavonic language and her
Western sympathies."[3] Like his father—high in government office—
the schoolboy René Wellek identified with the new Czechoslovakia.
"The outcome of the great war, which for the Czechs meant the
fulfillment of a centuries-old desire, was a surprise and shock for
the Germans in Bohemia and Moravia."[4] Still, the first president
of the Republic, Thomas Masaryk, hoped that Czechoslovakia might
become the Switzerland of Central Europe.

No English, however, was taught at Wellek's *Realgymnasium*.
Nevertheless, he continued to read English literature at home, particularly Shakespeare and the Romantic poets. In school he studied
botany, history, geography, and three literatures—Latin, German,
and Czech. He read a good deal of Reformation history and became
familiar with the German classics. After reading Schopenhauer and
Nietzsche, he puzzled over his mother's sentimental piety.

In 1922, Wellek entered Charles University (the Czech University
of Prague). Though he viewed his father's legal profession as boring,
he himself would become a masterful judge of evidence, of critical
defense and prosecution. Wellek prevailed upon his father to allow
him to study Germanic philology. Academe promised intellectual
adventure and social responsibility, art and learning, passion and
judgment. At Charles University, German historical scholarship still
held sway, but often it collaborated with criticism. Joseph Janko
lectured on Gothic vocalism and consonantism, Arnošt Kraus on the
Minnesänger, Otokar Fischer on the life and poetry of Heine, F.
X. Šalda on Symbolism, and Václav Tille on comparative folklore.
From each Wellek learned, but from each he withheld total allegiance. Fascinated by the judgmental boldness of Friedrich Gundolf's *Shakespeare und der deutsche Geist* (1911) and *Goethe* (1916),
Wellek in 1923 visited Heidelberg to hear Gundolf lecture; after
calling on him, however, Wellek was repelled by Gundolf's adoring
cult of Stefan George.[5]

At Charles University, Wellek enjoyed the lectures on English
literary history given by the highly regarded Czech scholar and

teacher Vilém Mathesius (1882–1945). The noble and polite Mathesius, Wellek later wrote, was "the type of the Czech scholar who
grew up under Austria in the tradition of Czech Protestantism, with
Masaryk as a model in mind, who devoted himself to the building
of the nation between the wars."[6] During Mathesius's sudden loss
of sight, Wellek (who then cared only for Shakespeare and the
Romantic and Victorian poets) read portions of *The Fairie Queene*
to him and observed that often Mathesius's responses to Spenser
went beyond the conventions of nineteenth-century positivistic philology. Mathesius, in fact, encouraged his students to free themselves
from fanatic German factualism and to write Czech exposition in the
simple, clear style of the English. Though Mathesius seemed to
Wellek insufficiently concerned with the problem of evil and tragedy, with irrationality and the interior life, Mathesius instilled in
him "a sane respect for order, tradition, common sense, lucidity
. . . distrust of the merely new, the pretentious and opaque . . .
a concern for genuine discovery, for the frontiers of knowledge."[7]

III *Wandering Scholar*

With his father's financial help, Wellek in 1924 spent two months
in England preparing his thesis on "Thomas Carlyle and Romanticism" and responding favorably to the Metaphysical revival. The
next year he and other Czech students, under the auspices of the
British Union of students, visited Cambridge, Birmingham, Liv-
erpool, Oxford, Bristol, and London. As an undergraduate Wellek
began publishing his efforts in Czech books and periodicals. His
first essay, in Fischer and Šalda's review *Kritika*, took to task J. V.
Sládek's Czech translation of *Romeo and Juliet*.[8] Other early essays
are on Byron and Shelley, early reviews on various studies in Czech,
English, French, and German. Under Mathesius, Wellek completed
his thesis on Carlyle: Wellek argues that Carlyle fought the Enlightenment with weapons from German Romanticism, but remained a Puritan. In June 1926, at age twenty-three, Wellek
received the degree Doctor of Philology.

Supported by the Czech Ministry of Education, Wellek once more
visited England, this time to prepare a monograph on Andrew Marvell in relation to Baroque and Latin poetry. But at Oxford, where
he met Mario Praz, Wellek was surprised to learn that the French
scholar Pierre Legouis was preparing a large book on Marvell. With
recommendations from Oxford, Wellek applied to the Institute of

International Education, and in the fall of 1927 he went to Princeton as a Procter Fellow of English. He spent a busy year in the regular graduate seminars of Thomas M. Parrott, Robert K. Root, Charles G. Osgood, and Morris W. Croll. Unfortunately, Wellek's seminar assignments were much like those of his early years in Germanic philology. At the time, Princeton offered no modern or American literature. Wellek, however, managed to read H. L. Mencken, Van Wyck Brooks, and the New Humanists.[9]

Since there was no opening for him at Prague, Wellek remained in the United States and taught German the next year at Smith College. The following year he returned to Princeton to teach German. Having avoided at Prague the professors of positivistic philosophy, at Princeton he attended Ledger Wood's seminar on Hegel's *Logic*. Wellek's thesis on Carlyle had led him to Coleridge, and Coleridge led him to Kant and Schelling. During this period, Wellek decided that the topic of his second thesis *(Habilitation)* would be the influence of Kant on English thought. Wellek then voyaged home by way of England. At the British Museum he scrutinized Coleridge's manuscript "Logic," amazed to see the fair and unfair use Coleridge made of Kant.

IV   Privatdozent

Back at Charles University by the fall of 1930, Wellek completed *Immanuel Kant in England: 1793–1838*. Though Mathesius had reservations about the subject of the *Habilitation*, he advised Wellek to enhance his chances of securing a professorship by writing a paper on the Middle English poem *The Pearl*. Wellek passed his *Docentura*, basing his inaugural lecture ("The Two Englands: Empiricism and Idealism in English Literature") on an entry in Coleridge's notebooks. Writes Wellek: "I developed the contrast between the two traditions with an unconcealed preference for the Platonic idealistic poetic tradition."[10] Still, Mathesius selected Wellek his eventual successor as Professor of the History of English Literature.

From 1930 to 1935 Wellek lived in Prague. He became an active junior member of the famous Prague Linguistic Circle, translated Joseph Conrad's *Chance* and D. H. Lawrence's *Sons and Lovers* into Czech, taught English as a *Privatdozent*, and wrote in Czech, English, and German for a variety of Czech journals. In 1932 Wellek married Olga Brodská, an elementary-school teacher from Moravia. Wellek early surveyed the work of the Cambridge critics—I. A.

Richards, F. R. Leavis, and William Empson—and contributed articles and reviews to *Slovo a slovesnost,* journal of the Prague Linguistic Circle. He further developed his considerable skill in textual analysis, formulation of theory, and reasoned evaluation. Believing that history can be written only from a sense of direction, Wellek as early as 1932 sought in his paper on "Wordsworth's and Coleridge's Theories of Poetic Diction"[11] for anticipations of the views of the Russian Formalists and the Czech Structuralists. Of great interest to Wellek at this time were the theories of Viktor Shklovsky, Roman Jakobson, Jan Mukařovský, and Roman Ingarden.

V *London*

Since prospects for a professorship at Prague seemed remote, Wellek from 1935 to 1939 was Lecturer in Czech Language and Literature at the School of Slavonic Studies of the University of London. Sponsored there by the Czechoslovak Ministry of Education, Wellek also gave six public lectures a year on Czech culture. During these London years, he contributed his important "Theory of Literary History" to the sixth volume of *Travaux du Cercle Linguistique de Prague* (1936, pp. 173–81). Wellek notes that this essay for the first time in English discusses Russian Formalism and Ingarden's phenomenology. Wellek argues against merely accumulating facts about literature, against reducing literature to historical information. He advocates concentrating on the actual works of art themselves, on bridging the gulf between content and form.

In Cambridge in the summer of 1936, Wellek for the first time met F. R. Leavis. Though Wellek's views in many areas coincided with those of the Cambridge group, his famous or notorious letter in *Scrutiny* in 1937 charged Leavis in his *Revaluation* (1936) with an inadequate appreciation of idealism as it descends from Plato, with underrating the coherence and comprehensibility of the Romantic view of the world.[12] Leavis wrongly countercharged that Wellek was an abstract philosopher with an inadequate appreciation of sensitive, concrete criticism.[13] Wellek replied that he had intended only to show that literary criticism directed against the soundness of thought is invalid.[14]

As Bronislav Wellek before World War I had transmitted Czech culture to Austria, so René Wellek before World War II transmitted Czech culture to England. Several of Wellek's thoughtful, factual accounts of Czech history and the Czech situation stem from this period. In London and environs, in speech and print, he sought help for his threatened homeland by acquainting the English with venerable Anglo-Czech relations, with Czech writers and values. Still, Neville Chamberlain, to Wellek's utter dismay, let the little country go. After Hitler's troops marched into Prague in the spring of 1939, the Third Reich halted Wellek's salary.

VI *Iowa*

American scholars came to Wellek's aid. Thomas Parrott informed Norman Foerster of Wellek's plight. Foerster, as Director of the School of Letters at the State University of Iowa, invited Wellek to join the English Department as a lecturer on a one-year appointment. Having ascertained the exact location of Iowa City on a map in the British Museum, Wellek and his wife gratefully sailed for America in June. Before the trip to Iowa, Wellek worked at Yale for six weeks on the manuscript of his *Rise of English Literary History*. The Welleks moved into a newly rented house in Iowa City on September 1, 1939—the day World War II broke out in Europe.

At Iowa, Wellek at first taught courses in the Humanities and the European novel. There he met several stimulating colleagues, among them Austin Warren. Reappointed, Wellek soon taught a seminar in German-English literary and intellectual relations. In the stormy debate in American universities between scholars and critics (history versus values, facts versus ideas), Wellek naturally supported Foerster's Neohumanist reforms. Like England, America lacked theoretical awareness. Its scholarship was antiquarian, its criticism impressionistic. To the collective volume *Literary Scholarship: Its Aims and Methods* (1941) Wellek contributed a revised version of his "Theory of Literary History." That same year the University of North Carolina also published his *Rise of English Literary History*. Wellek became an associate professor at Iowa and associate editor of *Philological Quarterly* (1941–46).

At meetings of the newly founded English Institute in the early 1940s, Wellek met William K. Wimsatt, Cleanth Brooks, and Allen Tate. Robert Penn Warren twice taught at Iowa as a visiting professor. Though Continental and American perceptions naturally differed, Wellek was impressed with these "New Critics." Sensing the limitations of New Humanism, Wellek and Austin Warren decided to write *Theory of Literature*, a book stressing the nature, function, form, and content of literature as well as its relation to neighboring but distinct disciplines. The needed book, surveying literary theory, practice, scholarship, history, and pedagogy, would bring together Wellek's insights into Slavic Formalism/Structuralism and Warren's into American New Criticism.[15] To expedite the collaboration, Wellek enlarged the scope of his reading in American scholarship while Warren read more European studies.

Meanwhile, Wellek accepted Louis Wright's invitation to work as a Fellow at the Huntington Library during the summer of 1942— on what Wellek imagined would be the second installment of his *Rise of English Literary History* (since Thomas Warton to the present). In the spring of 1943 Wellek's son Ivan was born. Because of the war Wellek naturally lost touch with the Prague Circle; nevertheless, he intensified his theoretical interests. At the center of his convictions were the autonomy of the aesthetic experience, the human meaning of art, the necessity for responsible interpretation, the interdependence of theory and experience, and the interconnection of analysis, interpretation, and evaluation.

As Director of the Language and Area Program in Czech (1943–44), René Wellek's function was to produce oral interpreters for the United States Army. He was promoted to full professor in 1944, but his grinding stint as language director had retarded progress on *Theory of Literature*. With support from the Rockefeller Foundation, however, Wellek and Warren spent the war-concluding summer of 1945 in Cambridge, Massachusetts. Enthusiastically the Czech and the American wrote, exchanged, discussed, and revised chapters. Of Austin Warren as writer and teacher, Wellek observes: "Working with him was a course in style, in the art of exposition, in the clarity of formulation."[16]

VII *New Haven*

In the fall they returned to Iowa, but Wellek, having learned Mathesius had died shortly before the liberation, considered returning to Prague. Yale University, however, offered him a post, and Wellek became a naturalized American citizen in May 1946. That same year Yale presented him with an honorary Master of Arts degree, and he joined the editorial board (1946–50) of the Modern Language Association.

Still working on *Theory of Literature*, Wellek in the fall of 1946 became Professor of Slavic and Comparative Literature at Yale.

There was no chair, no program, no department then, but Wellek sensed that the time was growing ripe for expansion.[17] Soon there would be 125 undergraduates in his Survey of the Russian Novel. Wellek rightly insisted that one cannot study a single literature in isolation. All literature is interdependent, particularly the literature descending from Greece and Rome. Ideas, forms, genres, themes, motifs, techniques, metrics, stock characters, and much more cross all language barriers. Professors of literature in whatever language or languages must recognize as an ideal the supernational history of literature.

Warren visited Wellek in New Haven the next two summers, but the illness and subsequent death of Warren's wife necessitated that Wellek write chapters originally assigned to Warren. Though *Theory of Literature* bears a 1949 publication date, most of the book was written between 1945–47, and it incorporates earlier papers, including Wellek's well-known chapter "The Mode of Existence of a Literary Work of Art," first published in the *Southern Review* in 1942. In the summer of 1947 Wellek lectured on literary theory at the University of Minnesota, and the next summer on the history of criticism at Columbia University, returning to Yale in the fall as chairman of his department. Meanwhile, Warren left Iowa for the University of Michigan.

Though not conceived as a textbook, *Theory of Literature* caught on in American graduate schools. In a short time, it became a *vade mecum*. Today it is an academic best-seller, in twenty-two translations.[18] Though the book often is associated with New Criticism, Wellek objects to being called a New Critic. Thanks to the fusion of the German-Slavic and Anglo-American critical traditions in *Theory of Literature*, students and professors of literature the world over have become cognizant of essential distinctions and of the cardinal idea that "a literary work of art is not a simple object but rather a highly complex organization of a stratified character with multiple meanings and relationships."[19]

To the first issue of *Comparative Literature*, on whose editorial board he is still a member, Wellek contributed his well-known refutation of Arthur O. Lovejoy's argument in 1924 against the unity of Western Romanticism.[20] In the summer of 1949, Wellek joined John Crowe Ransom, Allen Tate, and Yvor Winters as a Fellow at the Kenyon School. Following the publication of *Theory of Literature*, Wellek put his greatest labors after teaching and administration into his monumental *A History of Modern Criticism: 1750–1950*, a projected five-(now projected six-) volume *magnum opus* of modern critical developments, primarily in France, England, Germany, Italy, Russia, and America. The work would support or correct *Theory of Literature*.

VIII *Profession of Criticism*

Since mid-century a flow of publications has issued from Wellek's pen—books, essays, surveys, reviews, notes, letters—on European and American philosophy, aesthetics, and history of ideas; on literary theory, history, and criticism; on periods, developments, and movements; on style, methodology, and pedagogy; on critics, scholars, and—himself. His many reviews on American, English, German, Czech, Polish, Russian, French, and Italian criticism are crisp and balanced. His letters and comments in learned journals contribute to critical inquiry, to a sense of intellectual community.

In 1955, Yale University Press released the first two volumes of the *History—The Later Eighteenth Century* and *The Romantic Age*. "There is no other history like it," declared David Daiches, "none which combines its scope with its sense of contemporary relevance."[21] For Wellek's sixtieth birthday, in 1963, the Czechoslovak Society of Arts and Sciences in America honored him with *Essays on Czech Literature*, nine of his key Czech writings in English, with a bibliography of more than a hundred Wellek writings in Czech and on Czech/Slavic topics. That same year Yale published Wellek's more unified collection, *Concepts of Criticism*. These fifteen influential papers, dating from the mid-1940s to the early 1960s, define problems of method and periodization, set conceptual ideals, and measure results against literature itself. To Emerson R. Marks, "No available alternative to the structuralism which he propounds bears so well the test of literature itself."[22] Exclusive of about sixty items in Czech, the bibliography covers all of Wellek's writings to the end of 1962.

Two years after the publication of *Concepts*, Princeton University Press, having put its imprimatur in 1931 on the printing in Czechoslovakia of *Kant in England*, appropriately published Wellek's third collection, six essays under the unambiguous title *Confrontations: Studies in the Intellectual and Literary Relations Between Germany, England, and the United States during the Nineteenth Century*. Howard Mumford Jones pronounced René Wellek "the most erudite man in America."[23] When Yale in 1965 released the eagerly awaited third and fourth volumes of Wellek's critical *History—The Age of Transition* and *The Later Nineteenth Century*—it was welcomed as "the most comprehensive and balanced account of the history of criticism in the modern age."[24] In 1970, Yale published Wellek's fourth essay collection (and bibliography from 1963 through 1969) *Discriminations: More Concepts of Criticism.* Among many others, R. Gordon Cox pointed up Wellek's "vast range of reference" and "encyclopedic knowledge of critical writing."[25]

Like most flourishing scholar-critics, Wellek constructs his books largely from his essays. Often these are lectures-turned-essays, one reason for their directness and clarity. Nearly all forty-two Wellek pieces that constitute *Essays on Czech Literature, Concepts of Criticism, Confrontations,* and *Discriminations* were culled from academic quarterlies and scholarly books. One runs across his essays and reviews in the whole gamut of learned journals—from *American Literature* to *Zeitschrift der Savigny—Stiftung.* One finds first or second versions, whole or partial reprints, or translations of his essays in a host of collections, annuals, festschrifts, editions, and reference works.

Over his long career, Wellek has reviewed more than a hundred scholarly books written in various Germanic, Romance, and Slavic languages. His reviews display the range of his essays and books. Venturously, he has assessed a scholarly book on Old Korean poetry for *Comparative Literature,*[26] and even an issue of *Yale Literary Magazine* for *Yale Daily News.*[27] Most of his reviews, of course, treat works in English on modern Western literature and literary study. Wellek's reviews crop up in dozens of journals, many in *Comparative Literature* and *Philological Quarterly.* Wellek's ingenuity in carrying ideas from one book to the next, in constructing books from essays and reviews, and in informing these shorter forms, in turn, with arresting passages from his books (particularly *Theory of Literature* and *History of Criticism)* makes for organic unity, for coherence and continuity.

Though the gusto of the great nineteenth-century critical historian George Saintsbury is more intrusive than that of his twentieth-century counterpart, Wellek's work also has a definite critical personality. The personality reflects habitual diligence, patience, and tact. There is erudition and introspection, system and vision, openness and independence, reason and enthusiasm. Judicious, subtle, and sober, the persona at times is dryly humorous—as when Adam Müller seems to celebrate "sentimental pan-sexuality" when ad-

dressing lady audiences,[28] or when Friedrich Hebbel notes down
his and his wife's dreams "with the pedantry of a confirmed Freud-
ian,"[29] or when the few today who want to burn with Pater's gemlike
flame "are usually very young indeed,"[30] or when Paul Valéry simply
cannot compare period terms to bottle labels—"Pabst Blue Ribbon
or Liebfrauenmilch"—or when the word *critique* gives "a somewhat
superior air to a humble book review,"[31] or when "it may be reas-
suring" to know that statistically nonconformists are more aesthetic
than conformists,[32] or when one fails to find the word *classicismo*
in such obvious sources as "Milizia, Cicognara, Ennio Quirino, Vis-
conti . . . Canova,"[33] or when Wellek, having counted the phrase
"Widerspiegelung der Wirklichkeit" ("reflection of reality") 1,032
times in Volume One of Georg Lukács's *Äesthetik*, concludes, "I
was too lazy or bored to count it in Volume Two."[34]

Wellek's distinguished writings have gained him distinguished
honors. Particularly satisfying to the academic man of letters is the
honorary degree bestowed upon him by a jury of his fellow aca-
demics. Esteemed at home, Wellek the American comparatist is
particularly hailed among the international community of scholars.
In 1958, Lawrence College granted Wellek his first honorary doc-
torate; in 1975, the University of East Anglia, his twelfth. Between,
Wellek had received honorary doctorates (see Chronology) from
Harvard, Oxford, Rome, Maryland, Boston College, Columbia,
Montreal, Louvain, Michigan, and Munich.

Of course, an academic writer whose erudition is as gargantuan
as Wellek's needs financial as well as moral support, large blocks
of time for reading, thinking, discoursing, and writing. Foundations
and agencies have heeded Wellek's call. To receive a Guggenheim
Fellowship is a great distinction: Wellek has received three. In
1951–52, he worked on his *History*, first in New Haven and later
in Italy, Switzerland, and Germany. His 1956–57 Guggenheim enabled him again to work without interruption in New Haven and
later to visit Czechoslovakia. On his third, 1966–67, Wellek returned
to Italy, mainly to Rome and Sicily. Before, between, and after the
Guggenheims, however, others backed Wellek's critical labors. In
1958 the Distinguished Service Award came from the American
Council of Learned Societies. The next year he was Fulbright Research Scholar in Italy, in Florence and Rome. Grants from the
Rockefeller and Bollingen Foundations allowed Wellek to take another leave from academic duties in 1963–64. In 1972 he was Senior
Fellow of the National Endowment for the Humanities.

An inevitable outcome of outstanding scholarship, professorial charm, and administrative dexterity seems to be election to various professional committees and offices. Active in comparative literature sections of the Modern Language Association, René Wellek was also on the editorial board (1953–54) and the executive council (1959–60). At the time he was MLA vice president (1964), he was also president of three other associations: the International Comparative Literature Association (1961–64), the American Comparative Literature Association (1962–65), and the Czechoslovak Society of Arts and Sciences in America (1962–66). Except for the first ICLA Congress in Venice, Wellek has lectured at every Congress. Besides reading papers regularly at ACLA meetings, he organized the 1970 meeting at Yale.

Such repute brought invitations to lecture and to teach. And highly successful lecturing and teaching begat more invitations. Long before his retirement from Yale in 1972, Wellek from time to time had accepted temporary teaching assignments elsewhere. In 1950, he taught a weekly seminar in the Enlightenment at Harvard, gave nine guest lectures as part of the Gauss Seminar in Literary Criticism at Princeton, and became a Fellow of the Indiana School of Letters. (Still chairman of Yale's Slavic Department, he became Sterling Professor of Comparative Literature in 1952.) The next year, he made a return engagement as a visiting professor at Harvard. In 1961, a year after he became chairman of Yale's outstanding Department of Comparative Literature, he was a visiting professor at the University of Hawaii; in 1963, at the University of California, Berkeley; and in the summer of 1969, Fulbright Distinguished Lecturer in Germany.

Wellek takes pride in many of his former students. Those now on the Yale faculty are Peter Demetz, A. Bartlett Giamatti, Thomas M. Greene, Geoffrey Hartman, and Lowry Nelson, Jr. Others teach in leading institutions at home and abroad: among them, Edward J. Ahern, Konrad Bieber, Ralph Freedman, Frederick Garber, Alexander Gelley, Thomas R. Hart, Leonard J. Kent, Sarah Lawall, Stephen G. Nichols, Pier-Maria Pasinetti, Peter Salm, Priscilla W. Shaw, Anthony Thorlby, William Whalon, James J. Wilhelm, Frederic Will, and Eléonore Zimmermann. Some important American and European scholars (nondepartmental graduates) who have taken Wellek's seminars at Yale include Victor Brombert, Remo Ceserani, Dorrit Cohn, Arnim Paul Frank, Agostino Lombardo, and Klaus

Poenicke. Of course, many fine scholars studied under Wellek at
Prague, London, Iowa, and elsewhere.

IX Wandering Scholar Emeritus

After the death of his first wife in 1967, René Wellek married
Nonna Dolodarenko Shaw, a Russian émigré, herself then a professor of Russian literature at the University of Pittsburgh. In 1972,
at age sixty-nine, Wellek retired from Yale. As director of the graduate program in comparative literature since 1947, he had directed
over fifty Doctor of Philosophy dissertations, many now published.
Wellek once wrote: "I trust the company who have come from the
department have, whatever the variety of conviction they hold and
interests they pursue, at least two things in common: devotion to
scholarship and complete freedom to follow their own bent."[35] Indebtedness to Wellek has been expressed in the form of anniversary
volumes, special issues, dedications, acknowledgments, and ubiq-
uitous footnotes.

In spite of academic retirement, René Wellek's academic *vita*
continues to burgeon. In 1973 he was a Visiting Professor at
Princeton, and in 1974 he was Patton Professor of Comparative
Literature at Indiana University. In London that year, he became
president of the Modern Humanities Research Association. The
following spring, under circumstances far happier than those in
1939, René Wellek, as Distinguished Visiting Professor, returned
to the University of Iowa. In 1977, as Senior Fellow of the Society
of the Humanities, he conducted a seminar at Cornell University.
In 1979, he taught at the University of California, San Diego. Later
that year, at the opening ceremony of the Innsbruck Congress of
ICLA, René Wellek received the *Verdienstkreuz 1. Klasse für Kunst
und Wissenschaft* and in the fall was Walker-Ames Professor at the
University of Washington.

In America and in Europe the irresistible "critic of critics" still
lectures in his rapid, Czech-accented delivery. He continues to
serve on committees and editorial boards. His various studies and
defenses of literary criticism continue to astonish and inspire. Wellek's memberships in learned societies, it might be well to note
here, include the American Academy of Arts and Sciences, the
American Philosophical Society, the Bavarian Academy, the British
Academy, the Connecticut Academy, the Italian National Academy,
the Linguistic Society of America, and the Royal Netherlands Acad-

emy. At his 1978 birthday celebration at Yale, René Wellek defined as his central pursuits the completion of the fifth and sixth volumes of his *History of Criticism* and the revision of his early, still valid, *Kant in England*. When asked how he likes retirement from academic duties at Yale, the sturdy, indefatigable, white-haired scholar quips, "I enjoy it but miss my vacations."

CHAPTER 2

Early Work

RENÉ Wellek's numerous essays and reviews in Czech preceded, of course, *Immanuel Kant in England: 1793–1838* and *The Rise of English Literary Criticism*, his first two ground-breaking books in English. Wellek's early and particular interest in German-English-American intellectual and literary relations, in Czech culture, and in literary historiography continues to occupy his mind. The relationship between Kant's great philosophical system and the thought of the English Romantics grew naturally out of Wellek's early absorption in Thomas Carlyle and German Romanticism.

I *Thesis*

René Wellek's Charles University thesis—"Thomas Carlyle and Romanticism"—appears in English, in part, in *Xenia Pragensia* (1929) and in a revised version—"Carlyle and German Romanticism"—in *Confrontations*. Wellek shows that while Carlyle rejected the eighteenth century, he also distrusted and misunderstood the English Romantics. Wellek interprets Carlyle's negative views of, among others, E. T. A. Hoffmann, Zacharias Werner, the Schlegels, and Tieck. But Wellek demonstrates that when Carlyle wrote about Jean Paul, he often wrote about himself. More important than Jean Paul's influence on the quirky *Sartor Resartus* is the closeness of Carlyle's whole thought to Jean Paul's—closer than to Fichte's, Kant's, or even Goethe's. Thus Wellek sees both Jean Paul and Carlyle standing at the same point in the history of thought, "at the transition from the Christian philosophy of the eighteenth century to the new idealistic theories" (80).[1]

II   Kant in England

Wellek's passion for Carlyle led logically to a concern with Coleridge, Carlyle's predecessor as an interpreter of the Germans. Kant's influence on Coleridge, Carlyle, De Quincey, and others constitutes the substance of *Immanuel Kant in England: 1793–1838*. While Wellek's book was still in press in Prague, J. H. Muirhead's panoramic *Platonic Tradition in Anglo-Saxon Philosophy* (1931) appeared. Still, T. E. Jessop felt it "remarkable that we have had to wait so long for an account of the introduction of Kant's thought into Britain."[2]

René Wellek's *Habilitation* about Kant's introduction, reception, and influence in England during the forty-five years 1793 to 1838 illuminates that nation's peculiar intellectual condition. The literati who accepted Kant ahead of most professional philosophers increased the English appreciation of German literature. But literature aside, Wellek's weighty dissertation reveals his intimate knowledge of Kant, Kant scholarship, and Kant's influence in other countries. One English reviewer, lauding Wellek's originality, erudition, and style, declared: "The author, to our discredit and his glory, is a Czech."[3] Again, T. E. Jessop found Wellek's competence "astonishing," but thought rightly that the 1838 break-off date—the date of the first complete English translation of *The Critique of Pure Reason*—more bibliographic than climactic.[4] Nothing came of Wellek's plan to write a continuation.

Kant in England begins with the rickety introduction of the critical philosophy into Great Britain. Resemblances and differences between Kant and the prevailing Scottish philosophy is the burden of the second chapter. Wellek devotes the next to the Coleridge-Kant relation, still a scholarly hornet's nest. Somewhat less controversial is Wellek's survey of Kant's influence on other English Romantics. Before concluding, Wellek unearths two obscure Kantian enthusiasts—Henry James Richter and Thomas Wirgman. The endnotes—forbidding to nonspecialists—are copious. A special feature of the book is the appendix, Coleridge's Marginalia to Kant's three-volume ˅ *Miscellany* (1799).

Wellek meticulously argues that England was no congenial soil for Kant's arduous ideas. Self-sufficiency and insularity combined with small interest in Continental strife and the German tongue. Shallow notions of Kant, Wellek discovers, first reached England via Holland. A year after the Irish physician J. A. O'Keefe urged

34 RENÉ WELLEK

translations and interpretations, a disciple of Kant, F. A. Nitsch, published the first English book on Kant, *A General and Introductory View* (1796), "decent," comments Wellek, in spite of "sinful commissions and omissions" (9).[5] Among the few who attended Nitsch's London lectures, Wellek informs us, were the Kantian fanatics Richter and Wirgman. Wellek observes that, apart from Nitsch's pioneering mission, one F. M. Willich (a former student at Königsberg) published *Elements of Philosophy* (1798), a hodgepodge. Next, Wellek unravels the "curious medley" of translations in Germany by the Scot John Richardson and his unethical printer. Small wonder, declares the scholar-critic, that Kant's introduction into England should be so inadequate.

After convincingly analyzing the failure of Kant's early propagandists, Wellek brilliantly compares elements which seem common to Kant and the ruling Scottish philosophy. To illustrate the confusion surrounding Kantian thought in Edinburgh, Wellek reports the impressions of a pair of German students there, as well as Thomas Brown's misconceptions in the new *Edinburgh Review*. Wellek demonstrates his technical knowledge of Kant by exposing violent misunderstandings in William Drummond's *Academical Questions* (1805).

Wellek directs much of his adverse criticism of the Scottish school to Dugald Stewart, celebrated professor of moral philosophy at Edinburgh. Unable to read German, Steward relied on the errors of Willich and others, objected to the "novelty" of some Kantian distinctions, and introduced his own philosophy into Kant. Stewart remarks that "the passion of the Germans for systems is sufficient of itself to show that they have not yet passed their novitiate in philosophy" (48–49)—and Wellek, believing then and now in mind as active effort, replies across the generations: "Stewart's very denial of system affirms a system of chaos and incoherence . . ." (49).

Compared to the work of William Hamilton, James Mackintosh's treatment of Kant is "thin and general." Only Hamilton of the disconnected Scottish school assimilates Kant in part, but revives him negatively, as a destroyer of rationalistic metaphysics. Indeed, it is Hamilton (objecting to Kant's Reason-Understanding distinction) whom Wellek views as sceptical, as lacking faith in a higher reality.

The next chapter, points out Lowry Nelson, Jr., began Wellek's "lifelong concern with the multifarious mind of Coleridge, whose borrowings and occasionally concealed plagiarisms from German sources . . . are the subject of continuing debate."[6] From his scrutiny of Coleridge's two-volume manuscript, "Logic" (1822–27), *Biographia Literaria* (1817), letters, notebooks, marginalia, and more, Wellek formulated his remarkable discussion of Coleridge's use and abuse of Kant. Considering Kant the greatest thinker of modern times, Coleridge studied him deeply, if not fully. Wellek shows that the English poet-philosopher approved, for example, of Kant's subjective idealism, triadic organization, and intricate terminology; among other things, Coleridge rejected Kant's cosmology, dichotomy of matter and form, and denial of intellectual intuition.

Wellek grants Coleridge his station as the intellectual center of the English Romantic movement and as an outstanding transmitter of ideas. But Wellek insists on a fundamental flaw in Coleridge, one "which never allowed him to integrate his thought into an organic, individual, Coleridgean whole" (66). To call frequent attention to "Coleridgean German" Wellek relies on the propriety of "[*sic*]," but to describe Coleridgean incoherence, Wellek resorts to architectural metaphor: "a story from Kant, there a part of a room from Schelling, there a roof from Anglican theology and so on" (67–68). Whence does Coleridge's instability and looseness derive? From "an inability to think systematically" (68). As a philosopher, Coleridge lacks genuine eclecticism, the ability "to melt, to polish, and to blunt the edges of other ideas" (68). Like most Kantians of his time, he became, in the end, "a defender of orthodoxy, of resignation, a prophet of the end and failure of reason" (135). Why did Coleridge once think the reconciliation between metaphysics and Christianity plausible? Ernest Bernbaum charges Wellek with not asking the question, not trying to find the answer.[7]

Turning to other Romantics, Wellek discovers for most English scholars that Coleridge's friend Henry Crabb Robinson had come to Kant on his own, as a student at the University of Jena in 1800.[8] What T. E. Jessop found "astonishing" about Wellek's knowledge of Kant and Kantianism was the added "familiarity with the obscurist byways of our literature and an easy unselfconscious grasp of our peculiar mentality that betoken both considerable erudition and considerable imaginative sympathy."[9] In reviewing Robinson's obscurely published and unpublished letters and papers on Kant, Wellek neither magnifies nor repudiates their importance—though *Kant in England,* in fact, had its inception in Wellek's chance encounter with certain letters in Edith J. Morley's edition, *Crabb Robinson in Germany 1800–1805* (1929). In isolating a few "Kantian" passages from Wordsworth's "Excursion," he judges them tokens, easily squaring with the poet's disavowal of Kantian lore. Robert Southey paid little heed to German philosophy. William Hazlitt paid much—without much discernment.

Wellek's analysis of Thomas De Quincey's papers in *Blackwood's* and elsewhere reveals that De Quincey, even with his faults, knew Kant better than Hazlitt. Shelley intended to study Kant, Wellek reports, but never did. Thomas Love Peacock's *Nightmare Abbey* (1818) is "a fairly representative example of English common sense reactions against the supposed mysteries of transcendentalism" (182). German idealism had its strongest proponent in Thomas Carlyle. Though he used and misused Kantian distinctions, says Wellek, he did not "come close" to Kant's position.

The enthusiasts H. J. Richter and Thomas Wirgman—one a painter, the other a jeweler—are literary outsiders. Still, they epitomize for Wellek the idealist background of English Romanticism: a medley of Christianity, Neoplatonism, and Kantianism. Wellek discourses on Richter's little tract *Day-light* (1817), as well as on his letters about Kant in London periodicals. Disclosing anecdotes about the odd Wirgman, Wellek spells out why, despite familiarity with Kant, the jeweler's spate of articles and books is generally amiss—at times even fantastic.

Wellek attests to the entrenchment of Kantian theorems in English philosophical tradition in the late 1830s. He detects among English Kantians of the early nineteenth century a characteristic trait: the ability to place the great German philosopher in the frame of English tradition and orthodoxy. Coleridge, for example, saw Kant as a defender of the faith, Hamilton used him as an agent against rationalistic metaphysics, and Carlyle as a cat's-paw against the Enlightenment. Wellek's unsentimental valuation of idealism alludes to the spirit of Kant in a number of later English thinkers, thereby justifying not only Schopenhauer's prophecy that the transplantation *might* be an event of historical importance, but justifying the claim advanced by Wellek's book that "the transfer of Kantian philosophy to England *was* an event of historical importance" (262).

Clearly *Kant in England* exhibits Wellek's fundamental belief in reason and system as a stay against confusion. Furthermore, this first book illustrates his method of girding doughty appraisals with exhaustive scholarship. However, the relationship is at times inevitably imperfect, revealing something of a divided allegiance, something less than a full reconciliation between erudition and evaluation, scholarship and criticism. Wellek's early depreciation of error, at any rate, is plain. In "A propos de Kant en Angleterre," in *Revue de littérature comparée*, Wellek rejoined sharply to the only unfavorable review, a pointing out of minor omissions by a Romanian in Paris, Basil Munteano, who was preparing a thesis on the same subject.[10]

Though the anonymous reviewer in *Modern Language Review* claimed that the Czech's English was superior to the native English of many dissertations (and sometimes even achieved distinction), young Wellek, more sensitive than his reviewers to subtle deficiencies, prefatorily apologized for his English. To be sure, a revision of *Kant in England* would free it of transcriptive and typographical blemish, inform and balance it with five more decades of thoughtful scholarship, and impart to it the masterful clarity and flexibility of Wellek's mature critical style. But if no revision is forthcoming, even the original *Kant in England*, as Jessop hoped, should "be given a place in every philosophical library" (521).

III *Middle English*

In writing the medieval paper advised by Mathesius—"The Pearl: An Interpretation of the Middle-English Poem" (1933)—Wellek's purpose was utilitarian. His sole excursion into this field resulted from his reading Charles Osgood's edition of *The Pearl*. At Princeton, Wellek had studied Spenser under Osgood. Surveying *Pearl* scholarship, Wellek rejected fanciful biographical and farfetched allegorical interpretations. By consulting seventeenth-century folios, he disentangled the theological question of the status of children who died before baptism. By arguing that the medieval mind saw no contradiction between a figure's historical existence and its symbolic significance, he tried to clarify the question of the poem's symbolism and allegory. That the visionary infant becomes a heavenly virgin who instructs the poet about afterlife presents no difficulty to the literary imagination.

First published by the *Charles University Studies in English*, the paper later was discovered and praised by C. L. Wrenn and J. R. R. Tolkien at Oxford. In 1966 Robert J. Blanch reprinted it in *Sir Gawain and Pearl*. Affirming that specialization is overrated, Wellek believes that any humanistic field is open to the trained mind. Naturally, Wellek's learning from medievalists that his early paper

remains a sane solution to the poem's main problems gratifies him
enormously.

IV   Practical Criticism

One should note that the René Wellek known today as a great
theorist and critic of critics engaged in practical criticism and even
in day-to-day reviewing during his years in Prague. Himself a translator, his specialty was reviewing translations from English—trounc-
ing, for example, poor translations of Joyce's *Ulysses*, Conrad's
Victory, and Huxley's *Brave New World*. Besides writing long essays
on Blake, Coleridge, Meredith, Wilde, and Yeats, he wrote also on
Huxley and Lawrence, had a lively interest in current fiction, and
wrote informative essays on English and American books in Czech
translation (1924–34) under the title *What to Read?*[11]

Thus we find this curious inventory: Shaw's *Saint Joan*, Gals-
worthy's *Forsyte Saga*, Priestley's *Good Companions*, Woolf's *Or-
lando*, Lawrence's *The Man Who Died*, Powys's *Wolf Solent*,
Sitwell's *The Man Who Lost Himself*, Walpole's *Rogue Herries*,
O'Flaherty's *House of Gold*, Forster's *Passage to India*, Strachey's
Elizabeth and Essex, Aldington's *Death of a Hero*, Morgan's *The
Fountain*, Wilder's *Bridge of San Luis Rey*, Dreiser's *An American
Tragedy*, Wolfe's *Look Homeward, Angel*, and Buck's *The Good
Earth*.

Besides his elaborate contributions on Byron, Shelley, and Rossetti to *Časopis pro moderní filologii* (*Czech Modern Philology
Quarterly*), Wellek reviewed scholarly books.[12] Particularly interesting is his stringent and still valid 1926 analysis of the evolutionary
theory expounded by Louis Cazamian in his and Émile Legouis's
Histoire de la littérature anglaise. Wellek reviewed Mario Praz's
Romantic Agony in the Italian original, Oliver Elton's *Survey of
English Literature, 1730–80* and *The English Muse*, and he closely
examined Bernard Fehr's methods in *Die englische Literatur des
19, und 20, Jahrhunderts*.

When *Slovo a slovesnost* (*Word and Literature*) was founded,
Wellek contributed to the first volume a review of F. W. Bateson's
English Language and English Poetry, salient passages of which
reappear in English in his recent essay on Bateson.[13] Wellek also
contributed a long essay on the Cambridge critics I. A. Richards,
F. R. Leavis, and William Empson—in terms which match his later
views in English.[14] At this time he also sketched the history of

English literary historiography, a preview of his *Rise of English Literary History*, and an essay on the topic in *Discriminations*.
In another journal, *Listy pro umění a kritiku* (*A Journal of Art and Criticism*), he began his debate with the Linguistic Circle and the Russian Formalists. In his review of the Czech translation of Shklovsky's *Theory of Prose* (1934), he rejected the extreme Formalist position, no doubt an inconvenient fact to those who insist on viewing Wellek himself as an extreme Formalist. The same review carefully analyzes Mukařovský and Jakobson's history of Czech versification and their theories of literary evolution.[15] In 1934 Wellek wrote a long account of the International Congress of Philosophy held in Prague, an event which helped shape his development.[16] There Wellek heard Mukařovský deliver his seminal lecture—"The Work of Art as a System of Signs." He also met the Polish phenomenologist Roman Ingarden, whose *Das literarische Kunstwerk* (1931) impressed him deeply.

V *Czech Lectures*

Wellek's writings in English on Czech subjects belong largely, as noted, to his London period, 1935–39. His public lectures on Czech culture at King's College on the Strand formed the basis for his series of articles eagerly published by the University of London's *Slavonic Review*. His first critical article—"The Cultural Situation in Czechoslovakia"—was followed by "Karel Čapek" (1936). William E. Harkins, reviewing Wellek's *Essays on Czech Literature* (1963), called the appraisal of Čapek "sound and refreshing."[17] One of the first in English, it rates Čapek a major figure in contemporary literature.

Wellek stressed the flaws and beauties of the relationship between Čapek's technical devices and his philosophical concepts. The early stories, often derivatively sophisticated, culminate, however, in two fine collections. The theatrical *R.U.R.* (1921) and the gusty *Life of the Insects* (1921) begin the period of dramatic successes, utopian romances, skillful essays, and charming travel sketches. But Wellek emphasizes Čapek's mature powers, his colloquial tales, and his novelistic trilogy *Hordubal* (1933), *Meteor* (1934), and *An Ordinary Life* (1935). In each, the true story remains hidden, but becomes more concrete with succeeding interpretations. One is tempted to see in Čapek's fictional perspectivism a prefiguring of Wellek's critical "Perspectivism"—neither in relativism nor in absolutism is to be found the poem's meaning, but in accretion, in the history of its criticism.

In 1936, for the hundredth anniversary of the death of the Czech Romantic poet Karel Hynek Mácha (1810–36), Wellek wrote "Mácha and Byron" (1937), a descriptive article based on his long Czech essay in progress for an important symposium on Mácha. The Czech paper, "K. H. Mácha a anglika literatura" (1938), published by the Prague Linguistic Circle, refutes in considerable detail the then current notion that Mácha was a Byronist. Wellek demonstrates that the Czech poet knew the English poet only partially, first in German and later in Polish translation. Wellek's ingenious reading of Mácha's canon and notebooks reveals the poet's interest in Shakespeare and his use of details from novels by Walter Scott and Bulwer-Lytton.

In the version for *Essays on Czech Literature* (1963), Wellek translated the Czech paper and conflated it with the original English paper. The yoking in "Mácha and English Literature" is somewhat awkward, not alone for the few distracting repetitions, but for its divided intention. What begins in general rhapsody ends in specialized scrutiny. Since the collection was meant, in part, for professional Slavicists, Wellek felt free to incorporate arguments of interest only to specialists. Granting the pervasive influence of German Romanticism on Mácha, Wellek nevertheless pronounces him as distinct, as original, as Vigny, Leopardi, Heine, and Pushkin.

As events were preparing the Munich crisis, Wellek could not escape political and historical questions. In "Germans and Czechs in Bohemia" (1937)—with what Peter Demetz described as "a fairness undiminished by the moment"—Wellek showed that in spite of periods of rivalry and strife, close ties have existed between these two peoples since the sixth century. "The Germans shared the fortunes of Bohemia with the Czechs in good times and bad" (79–80). While noting the feuds, Wellek exemplified German-Czech collaboration and hinted that their most palpable difference was linguistic. Clearly, both Bohemia and Wellek had absorbed and distinctively modified influences from both West and East, with Germany as their chief Western mediator. During this period, Wellek reviewed Konrad Bittner's extremely biased, pro-Nazi *Deutsche und Tschechen*.[18]

In preparing lectures for his English audience (and the Czech colony in London), Wellek thought that an account of what Englishmen knew of Bohemia might be of interest. He plunged into extensive research in the British Museum and elsewhere. With little help from earlier studies, he was able to assemble many travel reports from the sixteenth, seventeenth, and eighteenth centuries; to discover a manuscript, "History of Bohemia" (1619–20); and— teaching himself to read Elizabethan handwriting—to copy unpublished parts of Fynes Morison's travel diary on a visit to Prague in 1598. Some of these findings Wellek used in three short articles for *Central European Observer* (1937), but the bulk remained in manuscript until, during the war, he sent to the *Slavonic Review* (now published in America) "Bohemia in Early English Literature" (1943).

This expanded essay, the longest in *Essays on Czech Literature*, is reminiscent of the exhaustive scholarship and method of *Kant in England*, but was considered by B. R. Bradbrook the "best of its kind to be presented to the English-speaking reader for a long time."[19] Though long and laborious, this article does show that, in a wide sense, there is more to British-Bohemian literary relations than Shakespeare's well-known image in *Winter's Tale* about the seacoast of Bohemia. Surveying references and allusions since the time of King Alfred, Wellek notes that the English had few contacts with the Czechs in the eighteenth century, for "the nation was literally submerged in the middle of Germany" (127). Wellek observes in his last section that "in the early 19th century Bohemia appears in English fiction as a wild country covered with forests infested by robbers in the dim region of Gothic romance" (128). For his specialized purposes, Wellek here reads English literature as a social document, but he does not, of course, view it simply as a mirror of life: he knows and explains precisely how the fictional Bohemia stands in relation to the real Bohemia.

In "Twenty Years of Czech Literature: 1918–1938" (1939) Wellek coolly and judicially described how, in the postwar optimistic expansion and democratization, historical romance, village novel, and old psychological narrative gave ground to folk song, free verse, and detective story. German literary influence yielded to Russian, French, American, and English influence. (One recalls Wellek's translations of Conrad and Lawrence.) A crossroads nation, however, Czechoslovakia soon felt counterforces.

In adroitly balanced thumbnail criticisms, Wellek surveys writers whose roots lie in prewar times; next he represents postwar "proletarian" poetry, the opposing "poetism," and the new "spirituality." Though stages in the development of the swarming novel are less clear, Wellek mentions a number of social novelists. The *Times Literary Supplement* pointed out that Wellek's adverse criticism of

Jaroslav Hašek's famous *The Good Soldier Schweik* "will no doubt
disturb some."[20] Wellek also found the Czech theater disappointing.
Knowing that German occupation would alter Czech literature profoundly, Wellek the historian still did not predict. He stated: "Inside
the Western literary tradition Czech literature has preserved and
reasserted a very distinct character of its own" (45).

VI   *"Theory of Literary History"*

In his last years in Prague and first in London, Wellek focused
increasingly on the problem of historiography. He read German
theories on the distinction between the humanities and the natural
sciences: Dilthey, Rickert, Troeltsch, Meinecke. In 1935–36, Wellek planned his history of English literary historiography and—with
no knowledge of the American New Criticism—expressed his views
in "The Theory of Literary History," published in the sixth volume
of the *Travaux du Cercle Linguistique de Prague* (1938).

This paper is important not only because Wellek mined it for later
publications, but because it demonstrates that he held many of his
central critical opinions *before* he came to the United States. The
paper questions whether any literary history has been properly a
history of literature as an art. Wellek then asks how one can treat
literature as an art rather than as social history or a series of critical
essays. He then emphasizes the aesthetic function, the indivisibility
of content and form, the use of the term "structure" rather than
"materials." Endorsing Ingarden's analysis of the strata of a work
of literary art, Wellek next discusses the mode of existence of a work
of art. He rejects all psychological and intentional solutions, including I. A. Richards's behavioristic psychologism. Though we see
an object from our own individual point of view, we still see a
structure, argues Wellek, which has the character of a "duty which
I have to realize."

Wellek then criticizes Ingarden for trying to analyze a work without reference to values. Wellek conceives of "Perspectivism" as a
process of getting to know the object from different points of view
which may be defined and criticized in their turn. Structure, sign,
and value form three aspects of the same problem. Although Wellek
admits that the work has authorial and social causes, he rejects one-
sided dependence; rather, literature influences and is influenced by
these contexts. Since Wellek sees literary structure as dynamic—
changing throughout the historical process while passing through

the minds of its readers, critics, and fellow artists—the work of art is both eternal and historical. Wellek thus sees values as growing out of the historical process of valuation. Though he admits the difficulties of the parallel with biological evolution, he rejects the view that there is no development, only change. He distinguishes between two concepts of evolution: one from egg to hen, the other from fish brain to that of man. Wellek rejects Brunetière's application of the first to literature; the second applies if one sees development in terms of values. Thus the literary historian must be a critic also. Consequently, Wellek sides with F. R. Leavis against F. W. Bateson (who would disfavor criticism in history) and amends Mukařovský (who would recognize only the value of novelty). Pleading for interpretive adequacy in place of pure subjectivism and relativism, Wellek admits one difference between criticism and literary history: the former concerns itself mainly with individual art works, the latter with the development of literature. Finally, Wellek looks to the future, to the possibility of a real comparative history of literature, to more than a collection of facts on influences, migrations, and motives.

At the second meeting of the English Institute in 1940, René Wellek read his paper "Periods and Movements in Literary History." Here he surveyed the hodgepodge of period labels, pleaded for periodization based on literary criteria, and repeated his arguments from "Theory of Literary History" for an evolutionary history. Wellek conceives of "period" as a time section dominated by a system of norms—neither a metaphysical essence nor a purely verbal label, but rather a dynamic "regulative" concept. Wellek's pointed entries "Development" and "Period" accent editor Joseph T. Shipley's ambitious *Dictionary of World Literature* (1943), which, incidentally, Wellek closely reviewed for *Philological Quarterly,* commending particularly the entries of J. C. La Drière.[21]

VII   Literary Scholarship

Wellek's chapter "Literary History" in Foerster's collective *Literary Scholarship* (1941) is in part a reproduction of the *Travaux* paper, with concessions to American empiricism: the ontological situs of a work of art and the interpretation of works of literature as a system of signs are touched lightly. The new, earlier part of the chapter foreshadows the organization of *Theory of Literature*. The word "extrinsic," however, is not yet an organizing principle in contrast to "intrinsic." Wellek briefly discusses what in *Theory* he calls "Preliminary Operations": the search for evidence, textual criticism, bibliography. Complaining about excessive "external research," he recommends turning to the literary text itself, as in the work of Oskar Walzel, I. A. Richards, the Russian Formalists, and the Prague Circle.

Palpably, the *Travaux* paper shows that Wellek does not disparage biography, only simplistic notions about the relation of personal experience to fictional constructs and critical judgment based on biographical knowledge. Wellek develops the idea that there is a difference between using nonliterary studies to throw light on literature and using literature as a document in other studies, as in Lovejoy's atomistic "history of ideas," which sees literature as "ideas in dilution," as inferior philosophy. Though Wellek recommends sociological studies, he argues for the comparative independence of literature from social and political situations. Again, Wellek criticizes *Geistesgeschichte* when it assumes a unitary *Zeitgeist,* most elaborately discussed in "The Parallelism between Literature and the Arts" in *English Institute Annual 1941*. Wellek suggests work in the evolution of a single writer, a genre (despite Croce), a period, a national literature, groups of literature, and, finally, a general history of literature as a distant ideal.

VIII   The Rise of English Literary History

The Rise of English Literary History (1941), published ten years after *Kant in England,* was a consequence, one sees, of Wellek's feeling the need while teaching English at Prague for a history of English scholarship. His book, he hoped, might serve as a model for writing such histories for other countries. Though his subject was a particular national history, he tried to clarify problems and principles underlying literary historiography generally and also to illuminate the impasse in literary study. Reviewers recognized the importance of Wellek's topic and his adept handling of difficulties. With particular reference to Edwin Greenlaw's *Province of Literary History* (1931), Earl R. Wasserman pointed out that "scholarship of the last few decades made Wellek's study possible, a study which traces the methods of literary study from its crude beginnings in the Middle Ages, the slow growth of the historical sense, the accumulation of data, and the culmination in Thomas Warton's *History*."[22]

Imaginatively organized, this book has two parts: "The Origins" and "The Eighteenth Century." The first part has two brief chapters—one "The Middle Ages and the Renaissance," the other "The Seventeenth Century." The second part has four big chapters—"Ideas on Literary History," "The Study of Early Literature," "The Writing of Literary History," and "Thomas Warton."

Literary scholarship in the Middle Ages produced only lists of writers and titles, a few collections of short biographies, and rudimentary literary history in verse eulogizing Chaucer and Gower. Change came with Humanism, the Renaissance, and the patriotic search for an illustrious past. Later biographies, Wellek says, derive from the extensive chronological catalogues of John Leland and John Bale. Patriotism and Anglicanism prompted the Elizabethans to start the tradition of Anglo-Saxon scholarship. Though Caxton and his followers printed the poetry of Chaucer, Gower, Langland, Lydgate, and Malory, little other Middle English scholarship existed in the sixteenth century. The earliest substantial piece of English criticism is perhaps Thomas Wilson's *Art of Rhetoric* (1553). More significant to Wellek is Webbe and Puttenham's sketchy view of uniform poetic progress—*Piers Plowman* and Chaucer excepted—toward the glories of Surrey and Wyatt. A strong sense of historical literary process appears in Samuel Daniel's famous *Defence of Rime* (1607), but Wellek notes that the appeal is to universal law, the same law underlying the "defences" of Sidney and other Elizabethans. The only exception Wellek can find to the notion of literary stasis is Francis Bacon's ideal of literary history as part of man's dynamic intellectual history.

Seventeenth-century literary history lagged behind English political and ecclesiastical history and Continental literary history. Edward Phillips and William Winstanley laid the foundations of biographical literary history. From Winstanley, discarder of dictionary arrangement, Wellek traces the descent to Johnson's *Lives*. The development of true history, Wellek demonstrates, became possible only through the growth of biography, antiquarianism, and criticism. Rediscovery and revaluation of past literature fostered the spread of primitivism and the historical sense—the possibility of narrative literary history. But the seventeenth century unsuccessfully explained literature: first by climate, later by social forces. Wars were a particularly fine topic for peacetime writers, Wellek notes, and the close association of democracy and literature followed the Whig Revolution.

The idea of literary development over literary stasis meant in time either uniform progress or uniform decay. Dryden, comparing the history of poetry to the history of the human being, called up the ancient theory of circular progress (the germ of biological evolution) basic to Sir William Temple's historical theories and practices. "In the seventeenth century," says Wellek, "all these suggestions remained uncorrelated, unsystematic, with no proper realization of their consequences and implications" (44).[23]

The eighteenth century completed the process. To lay bare this complex pattern, Wellek describes the warp and woof sequentially, but one is to see "mutual interdependences acting in all directions" (48). In "Ideas on Literary History"—singled out by Wasserman as the finest chapter—Wellek traces the gradual changeabout in the arts from the general to the individual, from formalism to emotionalism. Biography revealed the poet's "originality." Interest in the poet's environment fostered critical relativity, toleration, and curiosity about early and foreign literature. Dogmatic assertions about the impact of climate on literary production gave way, Wellek shows, to obscure notions about the influence of landscape and political conditions. Questions about religious modes led to the great contrast between primitive and modern poetry—the former universal and sentimental, the latter rational and refined.

By juxtaposing contradictory quotations, Wellek makes one sensible to the age's confusion about primitive poetry. The belief that poetry is universal and primitive poetry uniform made possible the idea of a general history of literature, along with theories on the origin and evolution of poetry. In this connection, Wellek finely demonstrates that linguistics also shifted toward individualism and emotionalism. As the generic approach explained the origin of poetry, so it explained the origin and figurativeness of language. As in the history of literature, biological analogies led to the concept of necessary internal evolution in the history of language—the record of human evolution also. "The very same idea emerged in literary history; books ceased to be bibliographical items and became members of a series, of which it thus became possible to write, for the first time, a history that was not only a catalogue of books or a collection of lives, but the development of an *art*, an activity of a nation and of mankind" (94).

"The Study of Early Literature" is a bibliographical essay which Wasserman judges to be "too much or too little." Many editions which Wellek cites played no significant part in developing literary history while unlisted volumes—and Wellek himself acknowledges incompleteness—in university libraries and private collections did play such a part. Allusion to 300-plus titles in this chapter naturally clots Wellek's style. Still, Donald F. Bond described the chapter as "succinct."[24]

The Renaissance (particularly Shakespeare) was highly accessible to the eighteenth century. Textual criticism made for fresh readings, a discarding of platitudes. Unfortunately, however, readers in time wrenched Shakespeare's characters from his plays. Scholarship next embraced Shakespeare's contemporaries, successors, and predecessors—especially Beaumont and Fletcher. Though there was little independent criticism, there was enough material, according to Wellek, for a partial history of English drama. Many nondramatic Elizabethan poets were reprinted, chiefly Spenser—and here Wellek criticizes the celebrated (but false) parallel between *The Fairie Queene* and Gothic architecture. New editions and anthologies raised problems, the answers to which Wellek characterizes as "empirical, haphazard, and sometimes curiously compromising, hesitant and even self-contradictory" (104). Not meaning "to play Ritson to Dr. Wellek's Warton," Wasserman nevertheless takes exception to Wellek's view that Elizabethan prose received little serious attention.[25]

Pre–Warton eighteenth century, Wellek maintains, knew little fourteenth-century literature outside Chaucer, Gower, and Langland. Better known were the fifteenth-century Chaucerians and Scottish literature. "The fateful gulf between Anglo-Saxon poetry and Middle English was never bridged in the eighteenth century" (117). Romance poetry seemed primitive enough, but Provençal and pre-Renaissance Italian poetry was meager, even Dante. Poems from Arabia, Persia, Turkey, China, North America, Peru, and Lapland consolidated the view of poetry as primitive and universal. Such materials "awaited only the shaping hand of the genuine historian" (132).

Before Thomas Warton, literary history was sketchy, specialized, abortive. In "Writing of Literary History," Wellek surveys changes in eighteenth-century forms and methods. Verse catalogues and "progresses," anthologies, and notes and commentaries still flourished, along with assorted collective biographies. More critical than historical, Johnson's brilliant *Lives of the Poets* (1779–81) appeared after Warton's first volumes, but Wellek reconstructs from Johnson's *obiter dicta* his view of English poetic progress toward the ideal norm of Pope. Though Johnson's little digressions on literary history do not lead very far, Wellek nevertheless finds them worth mentioning. Then the scholar pulls together his various threads: "The history in verse was obviously remote from the purposes of scholarship; the collective biography, the isolation of the individual authors, was in its very nature antagonistic to a conception of the continuity of literature as an art; and the systematic elaborate commentary, valuable as it was for the interpretation of individual passages, blocked the way to general views and the use of historical criteria" (145). Political historiography incorporated some national literary history, but Wellek finds David Hume's judgments in his five-volume *History of England* (1754–62) disappointing.

Vital to the formation of a full-scale literary history were narrative histories treating a particular genre. Wellek cogently reviews such histories (and even some outlines) in drama, epic, and romance. Interesting in light of his later *History* is Wellek's brief survey of the "History of Criticism" in Pope's *Essay on Criticism* (1711), Blackmore's *Essay on the Nature and Constitution of Epick Poetry* (1716), and James Harris's *Upon the Rise and Progress of Criticism* (1752). Dr. Johnson abandoned his plan to write a history of criticism—a genuine loss to Wellek and literary history.

The highly integrated and climactic final chapter Wellek devotes to Thomas Warton (1728–90), who "knew practically everything that had been achieved by previous scholarship" (174). Elucidating Warton's limitations, Wellek yet defends him from abuse. Though no great critic, Warton was no mere antiquarian. Wellek's demonstration compares Warton's more contradictory *Observations on the Fairie Queene* (1754) with his immensely important three-volume *History of English Poetry* (1774–81). "Were the history of the history of English literary history ever to be written," writes Wasserman, "the parallel between the preparations for Warton's *History* and [Wellek's] volume would no doubt be commented upon."[26] Though Wellek approves of Warton's combination of historical method and critical discrimination, he points out Warton's shortcomings in construction and selectivity. Underlying Warton's *History* are the Neoclassical concepts of progress from rudeness to elegance and of Classicism as universal truth. Still, like other contemporaries, Warton appreciated Gothic extravagance, and he praised, for example, the medieval genius of Chaucer and Milton.

Wellek takes pains to show that Warton and others regretted their world's rejection of old mythology, the very stuff of poetry in its *first* or primitive stage. Like Richard Hurd, Warton saw Elizabethan poetry as combining reason and imagination—the *second* stage. Still, a rich poetry was possible even in his own *third* stage of judgment and correctness—if poets decorously reintroduced the picturesque, the fanciful. Warton thus is representative of eighteenth-century dualism: classical propriety and reason on the one hand, imaginative flight and original genius on the other.

Wellek ends his exemplary study with measured praise, with an extended summary of Warton's pioneering achievement. One should note that Wellek, here and in his *History of Criticism,* points to the ramifications of Warton's fondness for the picturesque: "There was much in this attitude that anticipated the future romantic interest in the mere trappings of medieval manners, and Warton exercised an influence on this point which was not altogether favourable to the future course of English literary history" (199).

Reviewers perceived some of Wellek's methodological difficulties—both in his completed work and in his intention to extend his history into the nineteenth century. Wellek's main problem, they felt, had to do with his organization and his explanation of facts within the chapters. R. Ellis Roberts noted, "There are a great many good trees in this wood of his, and he can discourse on them; but he hasn't the art of displaying the wood itself."[27] Less fancifully, Alan D. McKillop wrote, "The explanation of the facts is something over and above the facts; they do not yield it of their own accord, yet it is not at a far remove from them."[28] Wasserman asserted that Wellek was eminently fitted to write the sequel to *Rise.* Wellek even accumulated a mass of notes at the Huntington Library for that purpose. However, his strenuous teaching duties and prolonged work on *Theory of Literature* interfered. More important, he came to realize that literary history is part of the history of criticism. In time, he conceived of a far more ambitious project, one which in small part, at least, could draw from both *Rise* and its unwritten sequel.

"English Literary Historiography during the Nineteenth Century" (in *Discriminations*) reveals what would have been, in part, the method of that sequel and its content, from Robert Alves's *Sketches of the History of Literature* (1794) to J. W. Courthope's *History of English Poetry* (1895–1910). Drawing on his 1938 *Slovo a slovesnost* article in Czech, "Vývoj anglické literární historie," Wellek discerns four types of Victorian literary history: scientific and static, scientific and dynamic, idealistic and static, idealistic and dynamic. But the history of the *art* of literature, he concludes, remains a problem.

IX *American Slavicist*

After Pearl Harbor, René Wellek established contact with such American Slavicists as G. R. Noyes, Alexander Kaun, and Ernest J. Simmons. Invited by Simmons to contribute a paper for a festschrift for Noyes, Wellek wrote "The Two Traditions of Czech Literature" (1943), the lead article in his *Essays on Czech Literature*. Even sharper than the English idealism-empiricism duality which he described in his *Docentura* address in 1931 is the Czech version. Wellek, of course, sides with the view of literature as an art, the view of the Prague Circle, reacting against both the Romantic nationalists and Thomas Masaryk's religious-ideological view of Czech literature as the development of Protestantism and Democracy. Consistently rejecting the notion of a uniform time-spirit, Wellek concludes with the paradox that "the times of artistic creativeness do not coincide or coincide only rarely with times of intellectual advance and political good fortune" (29–30).

Very much aware of the political and ethical significance of Thomas Masaryk as a symbol of anti-Nazi resistance at home and abroad, Wellek wrote "Masaryk's Philosophy" (1945). The paper (in *Essays on Czech Literature*) uncovers the ground of this leader's well-known struggle for the liberation of Czechoslovakia and his seventeen-year presidency after World War I. Of interest to Wellek is Masaryk's combination of extreme empiricism and religious conviction. Wellek's philosophical portrait of Masaryk helped define the temporarily submerged Czech spirit.

In 1945, Wellek wrote for the *Columbia Dictionary of Modern European Literature* (1947) all forty-two articles on Czech and Slovak literature and authors. Often Wellek's short, factual characterizations are highly critical. So critical is his view of Hašek, noted earlier, that the editor replaced it in a new edition. Still, about half of Wellek's original entries remain, the other half excluded by an editorial redefinition of "Modern"—since 1900 instead of 1870. Wellek's entry "Czech Literature" appears in *Collier's Encyclopedia* (1950) and, much later, he wrote "Letteratura ceca, Teatro, Letteratura slovacca" for *Il Milione: Enciclopedia del Novecento* (1976). His Introduction (1948) to *Dead Souls* reveals the professor-critic's rapport with literature, the Slavicist's enthusiasm in teaching how to understand and enjoy Gogol.

X   *German Ideas in America and England*

Kant in England would lead Wellek inevitably to the question of Kant in America. Two papers—"The Minor Transcendentalists and German Philosophy" (1942) and "Emerson and German Philosophy" (1943)—appeared first in the *New England Quarterly*, were reprinted in *Confrontations* as the final two essays, and pronounced by *American Literature* a "valuable contribution."[29] The first essay examines the impact not only of Kant, but also of Fichte, Schelling, and Hegel on Bronson Alcott, George Ripley, Theodore Parker, Margaret Fuller, and on the Transcendentalist who understood Kant best, Orestes Brownson. Calvin S. Brown singled out this essay as "a model for study in the history of ideas."[30]

The second essay uncovers Emerson's tenuous relationship with the German philosophers. Like Carlyle, the intuitive Emerson looked to them chiefly as support for his own special faith, a worldview opposed to eighteenth-century materialism. Though Emerson often mentioned Kant as a moral philosopher and appropriated a few Kantian concepts via Coleridge, Wellek indicates that Emerson did not deeply penetrate Kant's texts and, like so many others, misconstrues him. Wellek nicely detects a Kantian passage in *Nature* (1836) mistakenly attributed to Plato—the same passage attributed to Plato by Coleridge in *The Friend* (1809). Native American Transcendentalism, Wellek concludes, did not adopt specific tenets of German idealism, should not be coupled with German philosophy, and should not be described as a result of German idealism.

Irritated by extravagant claims made by Sigmund K. Proctor in *Thomas De Quincey's Theory of Literature* (1943), Wellek showed in his essay "De Quincey's Status in the History of Ideas" (1944)—reprinted in *Confrontations*—that De Quincey's great contributions derived from widespread German discussion. Defending his own position on De Quincey in *Immanuel Kant in England*, Wellek contends that Proctor's "falsely intellectualistic approach imposes a conceptual scheme on a writer of artistic temperament and, at any price, extracts a system from *obiter dicta*" (150). A champion of scholarly polemics—of thesis, antithesis, synthesis—Wellek calls for perspective, for discrimination, for fearlessness in the cause of knowledge.

Ostensibly a book review, "Carlyle and the Philosophy of History" (1944) reaches conclusions Wellek earlier propounded. His point of departure in this essay (in *Confrontations*) is Louis Merwin Young's *Thomas Carlyle and the Art of History* (1939) and Hill Shine's *Carlyle and the Saint-Simonians* (1941). Unlike them, Wellek finds Carlyle's affiliations not with French sociologism, but with German organic historicism and eighteenth-century British writers. Like them, Carlyle stresses ineffable individuality, unpredictable development, intuitive interpretation. His portraits of Goethe, Schiller, Jean Paul, and Burns are superb. Shine's book exhibits for Wellek the error of investigating a theme in isolation, and Young's claims for Carlyle as a kind of Comtean philosopher are doomed to failure. Fearing the anarchy of values, Wellek praises Carlyle's moral insight, his ability to steer a course between blind faith in progress and blind pessimistic fatalism. In the midst of the Second World War, Carlyle's Manichean concept of a struggle between good and evil apparently appealed to Wellek.

XI   *Revolt against Positivism*

In his "trial" address at Yale University in 1946—"The Revolt against Positivism in European Literary Scholarship"—the Czech scholar from Iowa importantly outlined the twentieth-century reaction against antiquarianism, factualism, historicism, and scientism in seven countries. Referring to the sharp contrast between science and history in Wilhelm Dilthey, Benedetto Croce, and others, he stressed that literary study, like history, is not "creative" writing. Like science, it is a system of organized knowledge, but it has its own methods and aims.

In France, its aesthetic and critical sense intact, the revolt was easy. In Italy, the idealist Croce transformed literary studies. England, suspicious of system, maintained textual criticism and the personal essay, but broke with positivism through close (often erratic) reading. In Germany, the fierce battle was waged among spiritual biographers, idealist linguists, historians of philosophy, cultivators of *Geistesgeschichte*, and racial pseudoscientists. Russian Formalism, an antidote to the revived positivism of Marxism, influenced some brilliant literary theorists in Poland and Czechoslovakia.

Though the former junior member of the Prague Linguistic Circle endorsed the close cooperation among literary studies, modern linguistics, and modern philosophy, he refused to relinquish the good in the older philology—perhaps an inducement for F. W. Bateson years later to refer to Wellek as "primarily an erudite *Philolog* of the old Continental school permanently in exile in America (first at Iowa, then at Yale)."[31] Indeed, Wellek and his friend Austin Warren wanted "not less scholarship and less knowledge, but more scholarship, more intelligent scholarship, centered on the main problems which arise in the study of literature, both as an art and as an expression of our civilization" (*Concepts of Criticism*, 281).

CHAPTER 3

Theory of Literature

IN developing their distinct, coherent, flexible program, René
Wellek and Austin Warren incorporated into *Theory of Literature*
(1949), one should note again, ideas and passages from their earlier
publications. Particularly useful to Wellek were some of his essays
written between 1936–46: "The Theory of Literary History," "Periods and Movements in Literary History," "Literary History," "The
Parallelism between Literature and the Arts," and "The Revolt
against Positivism." As well as bringing the splendid bibliography
up to date, the second and third editions of *Theory of Literature*
(1956 and 1962) include a few corrections and clarifications based
on ideas which Wellek developed in some of his later essays on
periods, style, comparative literature, and American scholarship.

Whatever their specific notions about *Theory of Literature*, critics
at home and abroad generally divide between the approvers and the
disapprovers of theory, between those who fear confusion and those
who fear dogma. Harry Levin accurately prophesied that *Theory of
Literature* would do for graduate programs what *Understanding
Poetry* (1938) by Cleanth Brooks and Robert Penn Warren did for
undergraduate studies.[1] *Theory of Literature*, Donald Stauffer declared in the *New York Times Book Review*, should be read not only
by graduate students, but "by every reader to whom literature is
more than an idle pastime."[2] Though *Saturday Review of Literature*
deemed the book "indispensable,"[3] some reviewers considered the
book too difficult, even for serious readers. Some readers thought
the book at times too hard, at times too easy. Aldo Scaglione thought
that the collaborators, by worrying about the layman, avoided precise terminology or used it carelessly.[4]

Theory of Literature crystallized a movement that had been un-
derway in America for two decades: the attempt to join criticism
and scholarship, the literary and the academic, the avant-garde and

philology. Harry Levin pointed out that while Wellek and Warren were with the New Critics at the Kenyon School, they also held offices in the Modern Language Association. "The campaigns are over," declared Herbert S. Benjamin, "the authors and those who subscribe to their theory are in full possession of the field, the important professional chairs, and the critical organs; it remained but to clarify the issues, autoptize [*sic*] the foes."[5] However, pro-theorist Eliseo Vivas indicted Wellek and Warren as "theorists without theory"[6]— a view which Scaglione regarded as "preposterous," inasmuch as the authors "seek a common foundation . . . by invoking the most valid traditions."[7] William K. Wimsatt, Jr., praised the book's clear theoretical vision,[8] while Seymour Betsky condemned its lack of a "controlling purpose."[9]

Reviewers divided over whether *Theory of Literature* asked or answered questions. Betsky, for example, referred to the book as a *"tour de force* of literary problems,"[10] while Donald Stauffer felt that it gave answers. Wimsatt indicated that the book offered students of critical problems something like the orientation and checks formerly available only to historical inquiry. Again, Stauffer admired the book's intelligent and liberal order, range, and purpose, but not all reviewers were happy with its synchronic organization into groups of problems. Levin, among others, felt that the approach distorted literature from an historical viewpoint, particularly earlier periods. Nonphilosophical critics like Betsky—in the school of L. C. Knights and F. R. Leavis—resented the book's lack of specific treatment and firsthand judgment of literary art. Some reviewers like Benjamin felt that Wellek and Warren exposed other theories until their own "mouse of theory" remained.

Rejected by the University of North Carolina Press, *Theory of Literature* finally was accepted by Harcourt, Brace. As it now stands, the book consists of four parts: "Definitions and Distinctions," "Preliminary Operations," "The Extrinsic Approach to the Study of Literature," and "The Intrinsic Study of Literature." The formidable Notes and Bibliography divide equally about a fourth of the book. In the first edition, the call for reform, "The Study of Literature in the Graduate School," appears as Part Five, deemed no longer necessary in later editions. Of the five chapters in Part One, René Wellek wrote four: "Literature and Literary Study" (i), "The Nature of Literature" (ii), "Literary Theory, Criticism, and History" (iv), and "General, Comparative, and National Literature" (v). Austin Warren wrote the third chapter, "The Function of Literature."

When the collaborators wrote their book, they did not know Wolfgang Kayser's vaguely similar *Sprachliches Kunstwerk* (1948), published just a few months before *Theory of Literature*.

I *Definitions and Distinctions*

Though perfectly aware of transitional genres, Wellek opens *Theory of Literature* with his common-sense distinction between literature and literary study. Wellek asserts the rational nature of the
latter. But how do we study literature? Though the natural sciences
raise interesting questions, Wellek views the application of scientific
methodology to literary criticism as generally disappointing. Ultimately, Wellek asserts—as he asserted in his "Revolt against Positivism" address—the methods and aims of the sciences and the
humanities differ. Rejecting general laws in literature as failures and
viewing factualism and impressionism as extremes, Wellek argues
for the value of individuality. A theory of literature, an organon of
methods, fosters literary knowledge and speculation. Of course,
literary knowledge rests on a vital precondition: the enjoyment of
literature. Sympathetic understanding, however, is not a substitute
for literary scholarship—conceived not as scientific positivism but
nevertheless as "super-personal tradition, as a growing body of
knowledge, insights, and judgements" (19).[11]
    To give the term *literature* meaning, Wellek rejects, on the one
hand, anything in print and, on the other, the Great Books in philosophy, history, and theology as the subject matter of literary study.
Rather, literary study is to focus on the art of imaginative literature.
Building on Thomas C. Pollock's distinctions in *The Nature of Literature* (1942) among literary, scientific, and everyday language,
Wellek stresses the relative importance in literature of sound patterns and linguistic exploitation, the relative unimportance of narrow
propaganda and referential fact. In characterizing literature as
"imagination," "invention," "fictionality," "*Schein*," Wellek thinks
of Homer, Dante, Shakespeare, Balzac, and Keats rather than of
Cicero, Montaigne, Bossuet, and Emerson. Even before Bennison
Gray argued in his weighty *Phenomenon of Literature* (1975) that
the linguistic-fictionality definition was contradictory, Wellek had
expressed scepticism about defining a specific literary language,
except for certain kinds of lyrics.[12] Later, Wellek even felt that
"fictionality" is insufficient.[13]
    Thus Wellek sees epic, drama, novel, and lyric as *central* to

contemporary literary study—to the chagrin of theorists who would embrace as equal to the above rhetoric, logic, poetics, and other nonfiction genres. Wellek cautions that literature, however imaginary, features schematized outlines rather than exhaustive images. Clearly, he attends closely to the work of literary art, identifying his view with such durable but not unchallenged aesthetic terms as "unity in variety," "disinterested contemplation," "aesthetic distance," and "framing." The literary work of art—one recalls in spite of vivid appearances to the contrary—is "a highly complex organization of a stratified character with multiple meanings and relationships" (27).

Following Austin Warren's graceful discussion of the various historical functions of art and his corollary that the principal function of literature is "fidelity to its own nature," Wellek takes up the problem of systematic, integrated literary study: *theory* (principle, categories, criteria), *criticism* (concrete works of art), and *literary history* (conditions, relations, development). Wellek's final point is that each kind, though distinct, does not exist in a vacuum. An ideal philologist, Wellek pleads that the three "implicate each other so thoroughly as to make inconceivable literary theory without criticism or history, or criticism without theory and history, or history without theory and criticism" (39). We experience literature dialectically: theory and practice interpenetrate.

In some detail, Wellek takes to task those historicists (intentional reconstructionists and empathetic relativists) who detrimentally isolate their methods. For Wellek, a poem's meaning is in its accretions, in the history of its criticism. Warning against false relativism and false absolutism, he suggests instead "Perspectivism"— a term appropriated from Ortega y Gasset, but one which Willard Thorp would equate with the painter's science of perspective.[14] For Wellek, all literature should be seen as one, as both "eternal" and "historical." Thus he urges the study of contemporary literature, as well as the application of modern aesthetic sensibility to medieval literature.

Finding the right term for his ideal of literary study is vexing. Wellek makes plain the pros and cons of "comparative literature," a term which at times seems restricted to the study of oral literature and folklore or the study of the relationships between two or more literatures—as established by Fernand Baldensperger and the *Revue de littérature comparée* and partly exemplified in Wellek's own *Kant in England*.[15] "Comparative" literature might well be identified with the study of literature in its totality, but to equate it with "world," "general," or "universal" literature also presents difficulties. "World" literature sounds pretentious, though Goethe meant by *Weltliteratur* some ideal union or harmony of all national literatures; for pedagogic purposes "world" literature often means simply the masterpieces of such luminaries as Homer, Dante, Cervantes, Shakespeare, and Goethe. "General" literature might focus on literary movements and fashions transcending national lines, but then so might certain "comparative" studies.

Though linguistic limitations are real, Wellek would prefer simply to speak of "literature," to think of it as a totality, and to see at least Western literature (and its Oriental influences) as a unity. He recognizes the value of stylistic, metric, and generic studies dealing with Germanic, Romance, and Slavic subdivisions, but he points out that critical ideas are international and that "the history of themes and forms, devices and genres, is obviously an international history" (51).[16] Critical of provinciality, Wellek deplores the lack of contact in America among students of different literatures. Central to Wellek's idea of literary process is the way a national literature enters into the European tradition. Obdurate Americanists balk when Wellek avers: "Universal and national literatures implicate each other" (53). Still, he has been attacked in the Soviet Union for "rootless" cosmopolitanism, for emphasizing the unity and continuity of the Western literary tradition, for not knowing Oriental languages.

II   *Preliminary Operations*

In their preface to the first edition, Wellek and Warren point out that *Theory of Literature* is not a survey of research techniques. To unite scholarship with poetics, criticism, and literary history, however, the brief Part Two, "The Ordering and Establishing of Evidence," focuses on those concerns central to the methodological manual, such as André Morize's longstanding *Problems and Methods of Literary History* (1922). Wellek warns against imposing on all students of literature a highly specialized textual criticism which, although necessary sometimes, is only *preliminary* to literary study. Bluntly, Wellek tells the student: "Literary works have been edited meticulously, passages emended and debated in the greatest detail which, from a literary or even historical point of view are not worth discussing at all" (57).

Wellek then discloses a variety of assembling and editing problems. In publishing old manuscripts, he advises selecting the manuscript nearest the author's own: "We plead not for modernized texts but for reasonable texts which will avoid unnecessary changes and give reasonable help by minimizing attention to purely scribal conventions and habits" (60). In matching a text with its presumed audience, Wellek takes up the problem of collected editions, as well as the tricky question of letters.

The rest of Part Two (drawing examples mainly from English, especially Shakespearean scholarship) treats problems in chronology, authenticity, authorship, and collaboration. "Collaboration," says Wellek, "sometimes poses almost hopeless tasks to the literary detective" (67). The collaboration of Wellek and Warren, however, poses no such problems, for the preface to *Theory* indicates those chapters written by Wellek and those by Warren. But the book, they indicate, is a genuine collaboration "in which the author is the shared agreement between two writers" (8). The revised edition eliminates some terminological discrepancies between Warren's psychological vocabulary (from I. A. Richards and T. S. Eliot) and Wellek's antipsychologic point of view (from Husserl). Again, Wellek notes that the kinds of scholarship discussed in Part Two—the material of which the English scholar Terence Spencer, for one, finds "disappointing" and Seymour Betsky, for another, finds "one of the better chapters"[17]—only lay the foundation for the analysis, interpretation, and even causal explanation of literature. "They are justified by the uses to which their results are put (69).

III   *Extrinsic Study*

In Part Three, "The Extrinsic Approach," Warren wrote Chapter 8, "Literature and Psychology," and Wellek wrote the other four: "Literature and Biography," "Literature and Society," "Literature and Ideas," and "Literature and the Other Arts." The authors mean by "extrinsic" those methods dealing with the setting, environment, and external causes of literature. Again, causal study, however valuable as exegesis, "can never dispose of problems of description, analysis, and evolution of an object such as a work of literary art" (73). The collaborators examine both modest and immodest claims for extrinsic studies. Perhaps too much has been made of their negative points. As for causal explanation of a literary work, they themselves prefer studies that treat the total setting—but they endorse neither *Geistesgeschichte* nor, finally, any viewpoint not relevant to "ergocentric" study, to study centrally literary.

One can judge the biographical method, says Wellek, for the light it throws on the development of genius, on the psychology of the poetic process, on the actual product of poetry. But how far, asks Wellek, is the biographer justified in using the evidence of the works themselves for his purposes? To what extent are the results of literary biography important for an understanding of the works themselves? Even when he can check life and work against each other, Wellek seems to regard affirmative answers with a jaundiced eye.

Distinguishing between such objective poets as Keats and Eliot and such subjective poets as Wordsworth and Byron, Wellek yet affirms the overriding power of convention and literary tradition. He rightly warns against confusing autobiographical statements with statements integrated into a work of art—into a unity bearing a different relation to reality than, say, a letter or a diary. Though biography can illuminate the tradition, sources, and material that helped shape the poet, Wellek sees danger in ascribing to biography any specially *critical* importance. Of no value to him, for example, is the criterion of "sincerity." "The poem exists; the tears shed or unshed, the personal emotions, are gone and cannot be reconstructed, nor need they be" (80).

Wellek's "Literature and Society" follows Warren's cogent but, according to the analytical Newton Arvin, "least satisfactory"[18] chapter in *Theory of Literature:* on the psychology of the writer, the creative process, and psychological types in literature. Among much more, Wellek treats the psychology of the audience. Experience tells us, says Wellek, that certain writers increase national pride, that the young particularly see literature as a transcript rather than an interpretation of life, and that many readers model themselves on fictional characters. Tradition and convention, norms and genres, symbols and myths—in these topics are important literary-social questions. Citing books on the effect of literature on its audience, he refers in his notes to the "brilliant dialectical scheme" (287) in Mukařovský's *Aesthetic Function, Norm and Value as Social Facts* (1936).

Discussions of "literature and society" usually begin, Wellek indicates, with the assertion that "literature is an expression of society." He maps the kinds of sociological data amassed about the profession of writing and the institution of literature: the writer's reputation, social provenance, and ideology; the chart of a book's success; public taste; patrons and the history of publishing; the role of critics, clubs, schools; and the isolation or the integration of the artist. Most emphatically, Wellek regards literature as a social institution, but of most conclusions on the *exact* relations between literary production and its economic foundations, between the writer and the public, and between the strictly literary and social change, he remains sceptical.

Commonly literature (particularly the realistic novel) is studied as a social document. Though social studies which view literature simply as a mirror of life have little value as literary study, literature properly interpreted can reveal social attitudes. But Wellek rejects the views of those who see a single social force as the "starter" of all the other forces. "The social situation, one should admit, seems to determine the possibility of the realization of certain aesthetic values, but not the values themselves" (106). Noting Marx's own insight into the *oblique* relationship between literature and society, Wellek finds Marxist criticism at its worst when it judges literature on nonliterary criteria and at its best when it exposes latent social implications in a writer's work. The third edition of *Theory* includes discussion of Georg Lukács, unlike the first edition, which limited discussion to the "vulgar" Marxism Wellek knew in the 1920s and 1930s.

Wellek can appreciate Karl Mannheim's "sociology of knowledge," but he finds its historicism excessive, its ability to relate "content" to "form" nil. He sees no conclusive proof of the social determination of forms, no real correlation between social attitudes and artistic values. "There is great literature which has little or no social relevance; social literature is only one kind of literature and is not central in the theory of literature unless one holds the view that literature is primarily an 'imitation' of life as it is and of social life in particular" (109). Literature, harboring its own justification and aim, is for Wellek no substitute for sociology or politics.

While declining, also, to read literature as philosophy, Wellek does not deny philosophical relevance to certain works of art. Some persons read a poem as a biographical, psychological, or social document; others would read the poem as a document in the history of ideas. In "Literature and Ideas" Wellek characterizes A. O. Lovejoy's method, at its best in *The Great Chain of Being* (1936). Like Hegel, however, Wellek sees the history of great philosophical systems *and* the history of philosophical concepts (Lovejoy's "unit ideas") as belonging to the history of philosophy. One sees clearly

the virtue of intellectual history in Wellek's own criticism, particularly in its integration of aesthetics. That literature reflects the
history of philosophy Wellek demonstrates by his myriad examples
of philosophical-literary studies in English.

As usual, Wellek raises fundamental questions. Is poetry better
for its philosophy? Are we to judge poetry according to the value
we place on its philosophy? According to its insight into that philosophy? According to its philosophical originality? To its influence
on thought? New is Wellek's exposition of certain ingenious German
speculations which too neatly reduce philosophical ideas and emotional attitudes to a few types of *Weltanschauung*. Since *Geistesgeschichte* (history of spirit) embraces sensibility as well as ideas,
Wellek suggests the term as a suitable alternative to "intellectual
history." But by now one is well aware that he rejects its frequent
assumption of a constricted coherence of *all* activities during a period. Though literary ideology often differs from artistic practice,
it is easy to overrate the integration between philosophy and literature. Thus Wellek invites the student of literature to address
himself to the question of *how* ideas actually enter into literature—
not to the problem of a universal history of mankind. In short,
philosophy is no substitute for poetry, and poetry is no substitute
for philosophy. "Poetry of ideas is like other poetry, not to be judged
by the value of the material but by its degree of integration and
artistic intensity" (124).

In "Literature and the Other Arts" Wellek glimpses studies dealing with mutual sources and influences. More important are literature's efforts at times to achieve the effects of painting and music.
Wellek does not dismiss the success of the Horatian *ut pictura
poesis*, but he feels that the amount of visualization and "melody"
heard in the reading of poetry is overestimated. "Collaboration between poetry and music exists, to be sure; but the highest poetry
does not tend towards music, and the greatest music stands in no
need of words" (127). The assertion that a particular poem, picture,
and piece of music evoke the same mood is for Wellek a vague
parallelism. Even less valuable are artists' theories and conscious
intentions, for in various arts they mean various things; also, they
say little or nothing about the concrete work contending with the
determining character of its medium. More valuable but seldom
analyzed properly is a comparison of the arts based on their common
social and cultural background.

The best approach would compare the structures of the various arts. The most concrete transfer of the categories of art history to literature, says Wellek, is Oskar Walzel's 1916 application to Shakespeare of the Renaissance and Baroque styles as defined in H. Wölfflin's *Principles of Art History* (1915). But when "severe" and "loose" structure is reformulated in the old literary terms of Classicism and Romanticism, the result is but one set of contraries for the whole of complex literary history. Wellek asks why the arts do not evolve with the same speed at the same time and why nations at certain times flower in only one or two arts—or in none. Each art, Wellek concludes, has its own evolution and internal structure, thus his rejection of Croce's aesthetics. The comparison of one art to another can be based only on their individual evolutions. The task of delimiting periods and establishing evolutions can be based only on evolving terms of literary analysis—on the evolution of a new poetics.

IV   *Intrinsic Study*

Compensating for the dominance in the world of scholarship of "extrinsic" literary study, Wellek and Warren made Part Four, "The Intrinsic Approach," longer by a third than the first three parts of *Theory of Literature* combined. Of the eight chapters constituting this principal section, each scholar wrote four. Wellek wrote "The Mode of Existence of a Literary Work of Art," "Euphony, Rhyme, and Metre," "Style and Stylistics," and "Literary History"; Warren wrote "Image, Metaphor, Symbol, Myth," "The Nature and Modes of Narrative Fiction," "Literary Genres," and "Evaluation." By "intrinsic" the collaborators mean, of course, the interpretation and analysis of literary works themselves. They view French *explication de textes;* German parallelism of the arts; Russian, Czech, and Polish Formalism; and English and American "close reading" as healthy reactions against the plethora of historical background studies, a Romantic legacy.

Wellek's paraphrase of a statement by Mukařovský in his *Mácha's May* (1928) touches the heart of the matter: "The Russian formalists most vigorously objected to the old dichotomy of 'content versus form,' which cuts a work of art into two halves: a crude content and a superimposed, purely external form" (140). Like the Formalists, Wellek and Warren consider the work of literary art a structure of signs, serving a specific aesthetic purpose.

In many cases the central theoretical chapter, "The Mode of Ex-

istence of a Literary Work of Art," has led to bewilderment or
misunderstanding, no doubt due to its rarefied novelty and referential compactness. Here Wellek returns to themes in his early
Travaux paper. To the question: What and where is the poem? he
disposes of several notions—first worked out in the summer of 1941.
The poem is not the printed artifact, though graphic print might be
integral to the total meaning. The poem is not its utterance, for
each speaker imposes extraneous personal elements. The poem is
not the mental experience of the reader, for different minds perceive
different poems. The poem is not the experience of the author, for
conscious intention and conscious-unconscious experience during
past creation are neither more nor less adequate to characterize the
poem than is the total contemporary critical situation.

Wellek defines the work of art, then, as a potential source of
experience, as an object of knowledge which is neither physical nor
mental nor ideal, but which one conceives as a system of intersub-
jective norms. As a "structure of norms," the "real" poem can only
be partially realized. Paralleling literature and Saussurean linguistics, Wellek says that the poem is to the system of language *(langue)*
as the individual experience of the poem is to the individual speech-
act *(parole)*. Still, one perceives in, say, the *Iliad*, "some structure
of determination." Through close comparison, one distinguishes
between recognition and distortion of norms, or among best, good,
and wrong readings. If preserved, the poem is a timeless "structure
of identity," but also it is historical and dynamic in that it changes
as it passes through its readers' minds. Upon their report of structure, sign, and value, one constructs a hierarchy of interpretations.

As for penetrating the work of art, Wellek accepts Roman Ingarden's ingenious method based on Husserl's "Phenomenology." To
no purpose, some theorists like Eliseo Vivas (as well as most so-
cioliterary critics like Irving Howe and Maxwell Geismar) deem
Ingarden "a bit esoteric for our public."[19] In *Theory*, Wellek made
fewer concessions to American empiricism than he did in his long
"Literary History" chapter in *Literary Scholarship: Its Aims and
Methods*. Still, to make the Polish phenomenologist more accessible,
Wellek consolidates the divers strata in *Das literarische Kunstwerk*
to four: the sound stratum, the units-of-meaning stratum, the stratum of represented objects, and the stratum of metaphysical qualities. According to this scheme, Wellek and Warren order the next
three chapters.

In "Euphony, Rhythm, and Metre" Wellek, expounding methods

hardly known in America at the time, focuses on the sound-stratum as integral to meaning and aesthetic effect. He distinguishes between the sound-pattern and the recitation of a particular poem. Also, he distinguishes between the quality of inherent sound (the individuality of *a* or *p* that makes for "euphony")and the relational or quantitative elements of sound (pitch, duration, stress, recurrence) that make for rhythm and meter—for "orchestration." Sound figures differ in effect from language to language and relate closely to the meaning-tone of a poem or line.

In directing attention to sound-imitation, Wellek steers a subtle course between John Crowe Ransom's dismissal of sound per se corresponding to sense and Maurice Grammont's "subjective" sense of the expressive effects of French consonants and vowels. Like Roman Jakobson, Wellek recognizes sound-symbolism and, referring to his brother Albert's account of acoustic experiments, speaks of the fundamentally different sensory meanings associated with front and back vowels.[20] "There is the general linguistic problem of 'sound and meaning' and the separate problem of its exploitation and organization in a work of literature" (163).

Problems of orchestration differ from those of rhythm—whether the "periodicity" of meter or the configuration of prose. Wellek distinguishes the leveling stress and pitch of artistic prose rhythm (which he defends when used well) from the irregular stresses of general prose rhythm and the isochronism of verse. As for the enormous labors expended on prosody, Wellek deems the gains small, noting among several efforts the vague theoretical foundations of Saintsbury's three-volume *History of English Prosody* (1906–10).

Here Wellek points out the merits and, what is new and more important, the deficiencies of the main types of metrical theories— "graphic," "musical" (which Wellek first encountered in Morris Croll's seminar at Princeton in 1927–28), and "acoustic." He speaks with approval of the nonsubjectivist Russian Formalists who apply nonlaboratory statistics to the relation between the pattern and the speech rhythm: they see verse as "organized violence." For Wellek, authors and schools fulfill ideal patterns differently, rhythmical bases vary from language to language, and the prosodic change is not prosodic "progress." "The history of versification appears as a constant conflict between different norms, and one extreme is very likely to be replaced by another" (172).

Characteristically, Wellek refers to a range of experts as he discusses the second stratum—units of meaning—in "Style and Stylistics." Like the previous chapter, this one supplies new information on the Russian Formalists, Czech Structuralists, and German *Stilforscher* group, with particular reference to the only work of Leo Spitzer available to Wellek at the time of writing. Though literature depends on language, Wellek sees the relationship as dialectical, for literature depends also on ideas, genres, metrical patterns, contextual aura. To be sure, linguistic science has its own methods and goals, but it serves literary study best when it helps disclose aesthetic meaning. While praising Wellek's achievement in crossing the language-literature line, the linguist Karl D. Uitti notes Wellek's "literary bias" and asserts that linguistic science "cannot be retailored into literary criticism."[21] Since stylistics attempts, among other things, to contrast the language system of a literary work with the general usage of the time, Wellek once more illustrates both the fruitful and the futile kinds of historical reconstruction for the literary critic.

Stylistics seems best to Wellek when it serves as the mean between the old disjointed study of rhetorical figures and the grandiose speculations on such period styles as the Gothic and the Baroque. Though stylistics should be neither prescriptive nor nationalistic, Wellek points to the absurdity of one behavioristic notion that all languages are equal, that a language without developed literature is comparable, for example, to English, French, German, or Italian. Among the European languages, a "comparative" stylistics, of course, seems possible.

Wellek suggests two approaches to the work of art: analysis of its linguistic system in terms of its entire aesthetic effect and analysis of its individual traits in contrast to comparable systems—again in terms of their aesthetic purpose. "Mannered" styles, he notes, are easier to characterize than "uniform" styles. Wellek cautions against indiscriminately combining stylistics with some of the earlier mentioned "primary" operations of scholarship, against viewing prevalent style as an "individual" style, and against isolating stylistic peculiarities without trying to formulate the principle of the artistic whole. Stylistic analysis, as Spitzerian linguistics brilliantly demonstrates, leads to problems of content, but Wellek remains chary even of Spitzer's psychological stylistics: "The whole relationship between psyche and the word is looser and more oblique than is usually assumed" (184). Finally, stylistics applied to one work or author naturally leads to groups of works, genres, movements, and periods—to the problem of the parallel between literature and the other arts.

Austin Warren in Chapter 15 impressively combines the last two strata—the centrally poetic image-and-metaphor stratum and the "world" of symbol and myth, with myth defined as a system of symbols. Thanks, in good part, to the influence of his chapter on narrative fiction, one today at least can entertain the possibility of amending Warren's opening statement: "Literary theory and criticism concerned with the novel are much inferior in both quantity and quality to theory and criticism of poetry" (212). In "Literary Genres," Warren surveys the long history of the problem of literary kinds. He takes his cue from Harry Levin, that the genre is an "institution"—like Church, University, or State rather than animal, vegetable, or building; one can express oneself through, can re-shape, or can create a genre. Warren treats the central problem of all criticism in "Evaluation."

While Vivas sees little relation between this chapter and Wellek's "Mode of Existence" chapter, Wimsatt points out that Warren places the problem of evaluation "in a very special focus for us."[22] Warren usefully distinguishes between value and evaluate, between aesthetic (Kantian) and nonaesthetic experience. The value of a poem resides in its degree of amalgamated diversity, its complex unity. (". . . The long poem today must 'do' in return for its space more than it used [to do].")

Critics like F. W. Bateson, who stresses reading as a temporal psychic activity, object to the special "immobility" of a term like *structure*.[23] But structure is where values potentially exist for readers like Wellek and Warren, the place where values are realized, actually valued, through aesthetic contemplation. Between overt and implicit evaluation—between a last-paragraph pronouncement and a detailed judging while analyzing—Warren (perhaps more than Wellek) favors the second method, the method of the early Eliot. Finally, Warren arbitrates the roles of sensibility and reason: "They exist in no necessary contradiction: a sensibility can scarcely attain much critical force without being susceptible of considerable generalized, theoretical statement; and a reasoned judgement, in matters of literature, cannot be formulated save on the basis of some sensibility, immediate or derivative" (250–51).

The first edition of *Theory of Literature,* as earlier noted, concluded with Wellek and Warren's postwar plea—dropped in later editions—for the reform of graduate study. Thus the conspicuous

last chapter—essentially Wellek's chapter in *Literary Scholarship*—
wrestles with one of Wellek's past and present preoccupations—the
problem of literary history, literary evolution, and the internal history of literature. In the late 1940s, several of Wellek's reviews
pointed somewhat harshly to the seeming unawareness of the problem of evolution in such brave and serviceable literary histories as
Grierson and Smith's *Critical History of English Poetry* (1946),
Baugh's *Literary History of England* (1948), and Spiller's *Literary
History of the United States* (1949).[24] Wellek describes most literary
histories as historical and not literary, or literary and not historical.
To isolate the aesthetic structure of a literary work and to trace
literary art in near isolation from its social context is indeed formidable. Only a few small-scale French and German histories attempt to treat literary evolution as an art. Like the political event,
the literary event is historical; but unlike the political event, it is
still *present*. As the "identity of structure" passes through new
minds, one recalls, the work of art changes dynamically. This change
is neither meaningless nor predictable.

With reservations, Wellek accepts as "historical" the concept of
evolution as a series with a beginning and an end. "The several parts
of the series must be the necessary condition for the achievement
of the end" (256). He assumes that by linking the historical process
to a value or norm, one preserves the individuality of the historical
event selected. "History can be written only in reference to variable
schemes of values, and these schemes have to be abstracted from
history itself " (257). The logical circle is unavoidable. Only when
literary works are seen within a scheme of literary development are
discussions on their relationships profitable—as in the question of
how one artist uses the achievement of another.

Wellek also remarks on some problems and exemplary solutions
to establishing a scheme of values for a series of works by one author,
in establishing some ideal type toward which the scholar can trace
a trait in a series, and in establishing guidelines for studies in themes,
motifs, genres, and types. Wellek himself, one knows, sees "period"
as "a time section defined by a system of norms embedded in the
historical process and irremovable from it" (265). The historian
should trace the complex rise and decay of conventions. And he
should give. literary names to literary periods.

An internal history of American literature would be a particularly
arduous undertaking: English is unconfined, the development of
literary art is incomplete, and that development depends on an

older and stronger literary tradition. As for the challenge of a history of a group of literatures or of a general history of the art of literature, Wellek declares that literary history has a future as well as a past. In closing, he sounds the worthy critical notes of comprehension, balance, and clarity:

If the ideal here outlined seems unduly "purist" in its emphasis on the history of literature as an art, we can avow that no other approach has been considered invalid and that concentration seems a necessary antidote to the expansionist movement through which literary history has passed in the last decades. A clear consciousness of a scheme of relationships between methods is in itself a remedy against mental confusion, even though the individual may elect to combine several methods. (268–69)

CHAPTER 4

Later Writings

FOLLOWING the publication of *Theory of Literature,* Wellek put his greatest efforts into his *History of Modern Criticism.* Besides the publication of the first two volumes in 1955, the second two in 1965, and many papers since on twentieth-century critics for the last two forthcoming volumes, Wellek has produced divers essays and reviews about Czech literature, Dostoevsky criticism, German Romanticism, comparative literature, literary theory, and, perforce, criticism. Important early Wellek articles appear in *Essays on Czech Literature* (1963) and *Confrontations* (1965), indispensable later ones in *Concepts of Criticism* (1963) and *Discriminations* (1970). Some important late papers are as yet uncollected.

I *Czech Papers*

Even before his presidency of the Czechoslovak Society of America in 1962 restimulated René Wellek to write again on Czech topics—on new developments in a nation dominated by Marxist dogma—Wellek, with Lowry Nelson, Jr., had translated from the German Pavel Eisner's *Franz Kafka and Prague* (1950) and Wellek had written the clear and direct "Modern Czech Criticism and Literary Scholarship" (1954). Here Wellek delighted in stressing the rare collaboration between criticism and scholarship during the time of the Czech Republic. Drawing on some of his early Czech reviews, he devotes half the essay to F. X. Šalda and half to Otokar Fischer, Arne Novak, and others. "These critics were professors and professors critics, almost as a matter of course" (179).[1] Interestingly, Wellek notes how Šalda, abandoning his *fin-de-siècle* mannerisms, developed a forthright Czech style capable of conveying his coherent and brilliant personality. Wellek's appreciative article on Šalda appears in the *Encyclopedia of World Literature in the Twentieth Century* (1971).

Wellek alluded to his 1954 paper on the old Czech guard in "Recent Czech Literature and Criticism" (1963)—the last article in *Essays on Czech Literature*. Wellek pointed out distortions in current Czech scholarship, particularly in the dull and rigid collective two-volume *History of Czech Literature* (1959–60), its general editor Jan Mukařovský. Though Z. Stříbny's *Shakespeare's History Plays* (1959) had its Marxist slant, the poetic sensitivity and analytical insight of its author gave Wellek hope that the life of the mind in Czechoslovakia was not completely dead. Meanwhile, the stout *History of Czech Literature*, playing down religion and Western influence, blacklists names like Roman Jakobson and René Wellek: "We have become," Wellek commented, " 'no-persons' from Orwell's 1984" (197).

The nine papers in *Essays on Czech Literature* (1963) presented by the Society to Wellek on his sixtieth birthday transcend the immediate occasion and offer, B. R. Bradbrook noted, a survey of the field from its beginnings.[2] Predictably, Czech reviews praised the early papers and disapproved of the later. William E. Harkins indicated that the essays "probe their subjects deeply, without any tendency to superficiality or popularization."[3] Included is a bibliography of over 150 items, Wellek's writings in Czech and in English on Czech and Slavic topics. "One feels," Peter Demetz writes in his introduction, "that these essays which are of more than purely theoretical importance reveal the scholar as well as the resolute defender of the critical and pedagogical traditions of Comenius and Masaryk; and one is tempted to believe that they relate, as few other of his writings do, to the vicissitudes of his life."[4] As a civilized man of letters Wellek, of course, acknowledges the practicality of the rationalist tradition, but Wellek the literary critic, one must never forget, responds powerfully to the aesthetic. Two similar essays, "Czech Literature at the Crossroads of Europe" (1963) and "Czech Literature: East or West?" (1969), argued that Czech literature belongs to the Western tradition: contacts with the West had been lively since the Middle Ages, but intimate contacts with Russia came late.[5]

Since 1967, Wellek has served as chairman of the Masaryk Publications Trust, established by the Czech patriot's children to bring to light abroad their father's suppressed writings. The entry on Masaryk in *The Encyclopedia of Philosophy* (1967) is by Wellek. Recently he wrote the substantial introduction to a translation of Masaryk's papers, *The Meaning of Czech History* (1974). Again,

while Wellek admires Masaryk's personality and achievement, he
tactfully disagrees with his antiaesthetic positivism—and with Remo
Ceserani, who, in a well-informed article in *Belfagor*, makes too
much of Wellek's supposed Protestant ideology.[6]

Wellek seems to be the first writer outside Czechoslovakia to
draw attention to the theories of the now famous Jan Mukařovský.
Naturally, Wellek deplores Mukařovský's later turn to Marxism and
his repudiation, as rector of the University of Prague, of his early
work. In his highly informative and relevant "Literary Theory and
Aesthetics of the Prague School" (1969)—originally a pamphlet published by the University of Michigan and later collected in *Discriminations*—Wellek meticulously traces Mukařovský's sources. "The
confluence of the technical analytics of the Russians with the speculative systematizations of the Germans was the decisive moment"
(279). Wellek describes and evaluates the best of Mukařovský's close
studies—in stylistics, metrics, semantics, and evolution—best seen
in *Aesthetics, Function, Norm and Value as Social Facts* (1936).
Referring to Mukařovský's 1951 denunciation of Czech Structuralism
as "public hara-kiri," Wellek yet admires the man's early speculations, making plain his influence and including a useful bibliography
for Western scholars.

In his original foreword to *The Word and Verbal Art* (1977)—
essays by Mukařovský translated and edited by John Burbank and
Peter Steiner—Wellek naturally alluded to Mukařovský's rejection
of his own early efforts. Yale University Press complied with objections from the Czech government agency controlling copyright,
but Wellek insisted that a Publisher's Note be added. The note
indicates that Wellek had hoped to provide a fuller account of Mukařovský's career between 1948–71, but that "under conditions of
the contract with the Czech copyright holder we were compelled
to delete this information, despite all efforts to reach an agreement"(xiii).

Though much of Wellek's most important work has been translated in such Socialist countries as Poland, Hungary, Romania, Yu-
goslavia, and even Russia, such is not the case in Czechoslovakia.
Still, Wellek openly professes his critical attachment to his native
country, as in his introduction to Alfred French's anthology *Czech
Poetry* (1973). Since he sees himself as a critic, not a propagandist,
Wellek risks lukewarmness rather than surrender his independent
judgment. He has criticized the choice of Arne Novak's *Czech Lit-*

erature for translation, and expressed doubts about the importance
of Prague-Spring literature.

II *Dostoevsky Criticism*

One reason for the ten-year gap between the appearance of the
first two and second two volumes of *A History of Criticism* was
Wellek's intense exploration into scholarship of Dostoevsky and
other Russian novelists. "A Sketch of the History of Dostoevsky
Criticism" (in *Discriminations*) appeared originally as the introduction to the Prentice-Hall *Dostoevsky, A Collection of Critical Essays*
(1962). Louis Leiter judged Wellek's collection "the finest I have
read in the series."[7] Other Dostoevsky specialists offered pet ad-
ditions and exclusions to the *Collection,* but found the introduction
"excellent" and "useful."[8] Wellek's sketch covers Dostoevsky's reputation, the criticism which he evoked, his influence on other writers, and the scholarship illuminating his work. Opposed interpretations
of Dostoevsky as social realist and Dostoevsky as prophet of the
apocalypse prevail in Russia. "The Marxists wrongly dismiss Dostoevsky's preoccupations," Wellek believes, "but the émigré writers—who correctly perceive the religious and mystical inspiration
in Dostoevsky's work—also misunderstand its nature if they extract
a message from it, a system of doctrines and precepts" (312).

This divergence is less marked in the West, but, again, Dostoevsky often is read from nonartistic points of view: existential in
France, philosophical and theological in Germany, psychoanalytical
in Central Europe. Expertly, Wellek details how Dostoevsky criticism became hectic in England around the First World War and
active in America after the Second. Exempt from either a Marxist
or an Orthodox interpretation, American scholarship increasingly
sheds light on Dostoevsky as a novelist, "a supreme creator of a
world of imagination, an artist with a deep insight into human con-
duct and the perennial condition of man" (326). Wellek is preparing
a similar collection on Chekhov criticism.

III Confrontations

The question of the relation between English and German literature in the Romantic Age stimulated Wellek, in 1963, to make
a formal comparison in "German and English Romanticism: A Con-
frontation," delivered as a lecture at the Conference on Romanti-

cism, Ohio State University, 1963, and printed as the introductory
chapter to *Confrontations*. As in his 1949 "Concept of Romanticism," Wellek parallels *Sturm und Drang* and English Preroman-
ticism. He indicates that personal contacts between English and
Romantic poets were meager. "Neither Blake nor Shelley nor Keats
nor Lamb nor Hazlitt nor De Quincey had any German contacts,
and those few that Walter Scott had were not with the German
Romantics" (8). Except for Coleridge and De Quincey, even purely
literary relations were slight. With the exception of Byron, English
Romantics remained unknown in Germany for a long time. Wellek
describes the common background of English and German Romanticism, and he details the divergent genre hierarchies in the two
countries. Byronic and Germanic Romantic irony Wellek relates to
contemporary alienation, even to discontinuity of the self. Incidentally, he shows that Eudo C. Mason's *Deutsche und englische Ro-
mantik* (1959) grossly exaggerates the mediating role of Henry Crabb
Robinson.

Critics of *Confrontations* recognized in the six essays Wellek's
assiduous research, brave efforts, and theoretical predisposition.
Without exception, they saw this latest retrospective collection, as
Inga-Stina Ewbank put it, as an "antidote to provincialism."[9] Wolfgang Bernard Fleischmann wrote: "This miscellany from the study
of a very great scholar has all the virtues which collections of a
similar nature often tend to lack: a lucid and readable style artfully
concealing mountains of learning, consistent evidence of original
thought, and . . . real organic unity."[10] Again, while Howard Mumford Jones proclaimed Wellek's apical erudition, he questioned the
critic's inclination to dwell on Anglo-American "imperfections of
understanding."[11] Tilling the same field here as Wellek, Henry A.
Pochmann sympathetically pointed up German-English-American
relations as "confusingly complex."[12] To liberate Wellek from "a
state of permanent deprivation," Louis Kampf bluntly advised him
to ignore *Theory of Literature*, to seek reasons for the change outside
literature.[13] Still, the intellectual history, the "nonliterary material"
in *Confrontations*, Calvin S. Brown surmised, would gain Wellek
a smaller readership than he gained for *Concepts*.[14]

Unperturbed by occasional charges of Germanophilia, Wellek
considers it a matter of intellectual honesty to recognize the origins
of ideas. Understanding nineteenth-century intellectual history requires study of Kant, Fichte, Schelling, Hegel, the critical movement from Herder and Lessing to the Schlegels and Hegel. However

deplorable twentieth-century German politics, scholars can neither ignore nor minimize the impact of German ideas at home and abroad. In relating figures and ideas to the main movements of the time, Wellek's method of history of ideas is empirical. As far back as 1926, Wellek, adept but disenchanted with conventional methodology, wrote on the social implications of intellectual history. Certainly *Kant in England,* however factual, is not positivistic and value-free, for it attempts to judge how this or that writer understood Kant. Thus Wellek's early studies in German-English-American intellectual and literary relations led to the question of the nature and unity of Romanticism—to the whole history of critical ideas.

IV *Distinctions*

In "The Concept of Evolution in Literary History" (1956), written for the Jakobson festschrift, Wellek abandoned the idea of literary development discussed in his *Travaux* paper. The essay, included in *Concepts of Criticism,* sketches the notion of literary evolution from Aristotle to Croce. Slavic critics in the twentieth century continued to grapple with the problem, but Aleksander Veselovsky divorced form from content and Mukařovský divorced literary history from aesthetic criticism. Based on implications in a paper by Yuryi Tynyanov and Roman Jakobson—"Questions of the Study of Literature and Language" (1927)—Wellek called for "a modern concept of time, modeled not on the metric chronology of the calendar and physical science, but on an interpretation of the causal order in experience and memory" (51).[15]

In "Concepts of Form and Structure in the Twentieth Century" (1958), Wellek recalls the reciprocity of form and content in Aristotle, German Romantic criticism, Coleridge, the French Symbolists, and De Sanctis. "Form" means different things, as Wellek ably shows, to Croce, Valéry, and Eliot, to individual Cambridge and American New Critics, and to recent German theorists. The result is "Babylonian confusion." It seems to Wellek that "in spite of the basic truth of the insight of organicism, the unity of content and form, we have arrived today at something like a deadend" (*Concepts,* 65). Russian Formalism exported to Poland and Czechoslovakia (in contact with the German tradition of wholeness and with Husserl's phenomenology or with Cassirer's symbolic forms) suggests a way out of "lumpish totality" or "atomistic fragmentation." Again, Wellek reminds us that form and structure cannot be divorced from value, from norm and function, from aesthetics and criticism" (68).

As a lacuna in scholarship induced Wellek to write his *Rise of English Literary History*, so it induced him to write "The Term and Concept of Literary Criticism" (1962), an exercise in historical semantics modeled on the method of Leo Spitzer. Using "criticism" as a point of reference for a history of ideas, Wellek also embraces contrasting and competing terms. In various times and forms the meaning of *kritikós, criticus, critique, critico, critick, criticisme, criticismo, Kriticism, Kritik*, etc., expands and contracts. Wellek's highly interesting and informative study offers convincing reasons for the replacement of "poetics" and "rhetoric" by "criticism"; reasons for the longer English form "criticism" in contrast to the Italian *critica* and the French *la critique;* and reasons for the confinement of *Kritik* in Germany to daily reviewing and the expansion of the term *Literaturwissenschaft* (science of literature). Though Wellek in his own *History of Modern Criticism* uses the contemporary expanded form of the term "criticism," he argues, of course, for the usefulness of the distinction between theory and criticism. Still, as Wellek's study in historical semantics demonstrates, literary terms are not quiescent: "We can help disentangle meanings, describe contexts, clarify issues and may recommend distinctions but we cannot legislate for the future" (*Concepts*, 36).

Playing devil's advocate in "The Poet as Critic, the Critic-Poet, the Poet-Critic" (1967), Wellek endeavors to explode the myth that the union of poet and critic is automatically good for poetry and good for criticism. On the one hand, poets like Dryden and Wordsworth seem unable to evaluate the work of other poets. On the other hand, Northrop Frye in his *Anatomy of Criticism* (1956) "spins his fancies in total disregard of the text" (*Discriminations*, 257), creates an elaborate fiction, an ingenious dream universe, lacking in ideals of correct interpretation, evidence, knowledge. To demonstrate what he takes to be the infelicitous union of poet and critic, Wellek the total critic, the specialist *par excellence*, reveals in ironic detail the "anticriticism" of Karl Shapiro, Randall Jarrell, T. S. Eliot, John Crowe Ransom, and Allen Tate. Dante, Goethe, and Coleridge are for Wellek not so much great poet-critics, but great poets at one time, great critics at another. Ben W. Fuson noted that Wellek's criticism on Frye is "devastating" and that "some may pause at Wellek's deft downgrading of subjective empiricist critical attitudes."[16]

For Wellek, concrete dialectics best limns the institution of genre. His somewhat technical "Genre Theory, the Lyric, and *Erlebnis*" (1967)—in *Discriminations*—criticizes arguments in Käte Hamburger's *Logik der Dichtung* (1957) and Emil Staiger's *Grundbegriffe der Poetik* (1946). Both try to assign "ultimate status" to kinds of poetry. The utterance of lyrical poetry is that of a fictive"I"—not, as Hamburger claims—a "real" utterance. Staiger's obscure existential scheme loses touch with actual poetry.

V   *Comparative Literature*

"The Study of Literature in the Graduate School" in the first edition of *Theory of Literature* indicated that "higher" literary education in America encourages nationalistic and linguistic provincialism, premature specialization, and pseudoscientific mass production. "American Literary Scholarship" (1963) points out that many of our schools still lack a theory to replace the demise of nineteenth-century German philological scholarship. "They seem to feel the need of reformulating basic questions over and over again, to start *ab ovo* to think on aesthetic and critical problems which have a centuries-old history" (*Concepts*, 311). Wellek recites his earlier pleas, pointing to émigrés Eric Auerbach, Amado Alonso, Helmut Hatzfeld, and Roman Jakobson as guides for young scholar-critics.

In later writings Wellek also elaborates the problem he had posed in his chapter in *Theory of Literature* "General, Comparative, and National Literature." In his review of M. F. Guyard's *La Littérature comparée*, Wellek attacked the mainly French concept of comparative literature as binary and factual. In his speech in 1958 at the Chapel Hill Congress of the International Comparative Literature Association—"The Crisis of Comparative Literature" (in *Concepts*)—Wellek broadened his objections to external factualism and atomism. Most particularly, he directed barbs at such influential comparatists as Paul Van Tieghem, Jean-Marie Carré, Fernand Baldensperger, and, of course, Guyard. "An artificial demarcation of subject and methodology, a mechanistic concept of sources and influences, a motivation by cultural nationalism" (290) seemed to Wellek symptoms of the prolonged crisis.

Comparative literature arose, paradoxically, as a reaction against narrow nationalism by those who, like Wellek, stood at national crossroads or on borders. Repudiating nationalistic "bookkeeping," Wellek (drawing on key ideas in *Theory of Literature*) called for an act of the imagination: scholars, like poets, should preserve and create mankind's highest values. Jacques Voisine recalls that after delivering this paper Wellek unfortunately "passed for many years, and not only among Marxist exponents of literary history, as the archenemy of all forms of historical research as applied to the study of literature."[17]

Even as a student at Prague, Wellek had rejected old-fashioned methodology, but now, suddenly, he found himself labeled an anti-French proponent of a special "American" conception. In two papers in *Discriminations*—"Comparative Literature Today" (1965) and "The Name and Nature of Comparative Literature" (1968)—he tried to disentangle the inflated misunderstanding.

In the first paper, his presidential address before the American Comparative Literature Association in Cambridge, Massachusetts, Wellek tried to create international understanding by reflecting on his own career. On trial for him was the whole enterprise of aesthetics and art. He pleaded for a balance between expansion and concentration, nationalism and cosmopolitanism, literature as an art and literature in history and society. Unwilling to overrate organizational machinery, however, he concluded, "The men or women struggling in solitude at their desks with their texts and their writings matter most in the long run" (54).[18] As of this paper, reports Voisine, a "Peaceful Coexistence of a kind had been established" between "historical" scholars and "critical" scholars.[19] But alluding to the North Carolina episode in *Revue de littérature comparée,* Jean-Louis Backès concluded that the best thing in *Discriminations* was Wellek's multitude of little facts.[20]

The second paper examines, among other things, "comparative literature" and, as in *Theory of Literature*, its rival terms. Drawing on his *Rise of English Literary History*, his *History of Modern Criticism*, and several of his essays, Wellek eruditely unfolds the main stages of comparative studies from the time of the Romans. In arguing against the sterile French method of mechanistic and factualistic causal explanation inherited from the nineteenth century, he reasserts his intentions: to help create a future for comparative literature, not a nationalistic squabble between French and American scholars.

VI *Periodization*

Clearly, much of Wellek's work is concerned with historical questions, particularly his papers written between 1946 and 1965 analyzing on the semantic model of Leo Spitzer the main period terms: Classicism, Baroque, Romanticism, Realism, and Symbolism. "The Term and Concept of Classicism in Literary History" (1965)—in *Discriminations*—recognizes the perennial appeal of Classicism. Tracing the history of the term, Wellek focuses on its development from one of valuation to one of style, beginning with the great Romantic-Classical debate in Germany. A long time passed, Wellek explains, before abstraction-shy English critics applied the term to the style of Dryden and Pope. During the nineteenth century alternate terms—"classicism," "classicality," "pseudoclassical"—were tried and dropped. Wellek is unconvinced by arguments of De Quincey, Taine, and others for the divorce between French and English literature of the time. "English classicism is, in critical theory, part and parcel of the huge Western European neoclassical tradition" (63).

The early "Concept of Baroque in Literary Scholarship" (1946) defends the term's usefulness in spite of ambiguities. Wellek shows how the term emerged in the eighteenth century as meaning "extravagant" and "bizarre," stabilized in the nineteenth century as a description of the decadence of the High Renaissance, and came to refer in the twentieth century to practically any manifestation of seventeenth-century culture. Focusing on the transfer of "Baroque" to literature by German and other European scholars and later by English and such American scholars as Morris W. Croll and Austin Warren, Wellek speculates on the status of the concept in each country.

While an American literary historian like Benjamin T. Spencer might wonder about the "use" of Wellek's analysis of the term's extensions, valuations, and referents,[21] Wellek himself concludes that "Baroque" best serves literary scholarship today when the term is confined to the conventions and style of a general European movement from the last decades of the sixteenth century to the middle of the eighteenth—and when the term itself means neither good nor bad style. "Postscript 1962" (*Concepts*, 115–27) proposes another etymological solution, notes dated statements, fills in gaps.

When Arthur O. Lovejoy, in his well-known essay "On the Discrimination of Romanticisms" (1924), claimed that the word "Romantic" had become meaningless, that we should speak not of "Romanticism" but of "Romanticisms," and that no one "clearly exhibited" a common denominator, René Wellek accepted the challenge. In his 25,000-word "Concept of Romanticism in Literary History" (1949) he discusses the term and its derivatives: and he argues soundly for the unity of Western Romanticism. While the English critic George Watson sees all this as "definition-mania," Aldo Scaglione declares that Wellek's disquisition "may some day rank as his greatest single achievement."[22]

The paper points up the common attitude of Romantics toward the imagination, nature, and language. Behind the many valuable individualities, Wellek discerns a profound coherence and mutual implication. Without an organic view of nature, says Wellek, belief in symbol and myth of import is absurd. "Without symbol and myth the poet would lack the tools for the insight into reality which he claimed, and without such an epistemology, which believes in the creativity of the human mind, there would not be a living nature and a true symbolism" (*Concepts*, 197).

"Romanticism Re-examined" (1963) reasserts the unity of Romanticism—its effort to identify subject and object, to reconcile man and nature, consciousness and unconsciousness. In spite of Lovejoy's avoidance of the term, R. S. Crane's impossible demand for literal proof, and Morse Peckham's initial verbal solution, Wellek finds growing agreement with his position in Germany, France, England, and at home. Still, Yale professor Geoffrey Hartman—who dedicated his *Fate of Reading* (1975) to Wellek and Wimsatt (*praesentia numina)*—"sometimes feels that if Lovejoy had written Wellek's article Wellek would have countered with Lovejoy's. The debate is a twenty-year standoff."[23] At any rate, because Wellek values national difference and artistic individuality, he tries to dissuade allies from calling him "the champion of a pan-European Romanticism."[24]

In "The Concept of Realism in Literary Scholarship" (1960), Wellek sketches the use and spread of literary (as against philosophical) "realism" and its competing, often alternate, term "naturalism," Zola's slogan, Wellek finds that Schiller applied the term to literature just before and after the turn of the nineteenth century. Citing the most authoritative scholarship, Wellek informs one that "realism" as a period term fares well in France and America, weakly in England, idiosyncratically in Germany, not at all among Italian Croceans, and all-powerfully in Russia. Though not bound to· past definitions of realism, scholars should not ignore theories and masterpieces acknowledged by the past. "Realism" to Wellek is "the objective representation of contemporary reality" (*Concepts*, 240–41)—

a polemical weapon (circa 1830s–1890s) against romanticism: the exclusion of the fantastic, the symbolic, the abstract, the highly stylized—the inclusion of the ugly, the low, sex, and dying. Wellek spotlights the illogical tension in realism between description and prescription, truth and instruction. Not Hegelian universal types (Hamlet, Don Quixote, Faust) but "social types" (seen by Marxist critic Georg Lukács as representative and prophetic) bridge present and future, real and social ideal—which led Alfred Owen Aldridge to remark that some Wellek here is "as entertaining as a satirical novel."[25] The criteria of the "absent author" and "historicism" advocated by some is for Wellek not indispensable for literary "objectivity." For Wellek, too, the distinction between realism and romanticism is more pronounced than between realism and classicism (Richardson, Fielding). Unlike journalists and documentarians, Balzac, Dickens, Dostoevsky, Tolstoy, James, Ibsen, and Zola created worlds of imagination. "The theory of realism is ultimately bad aesthetics because all art is 'making' and is a world in itself of illusion and symbolic forms" (255).

This conclusion caused E. B. Greenwood to announce that "one almost grips ones [*sic*] chair in astonishment."[26] Nevertheless, Wellek—citing three contradictory Greenwood definitions of realism, three misunderstandings, and one unfair misquotation—maintained his equanimity in the face of the professor's astonishment.[27] Wellek, incidentally, wrote engagingly on "Realism and Naturalism" in the several editions of the popular Norton anthology *World Masterpieces*. Here also he introduced masterworks of Balzac, Flaubert, Dickens, Ibsen, James, and his cherished Dostoevsky, Tolstoy, Chekhov, and Turgenev. (The novelists most dear to Wellek's critical heart are Dostoevsky and Gogol.)

In "The Term and Concept of Symbolism in Literary History" (1969) Wellek sketches another complex critical story. The paper, Jacques Voisine indicates, "is perhaps the first serious attempt to survey the movement as a period of European literary history."[28] Wellek focuses on "symbolisme" (Jean Moréas's name in 1885 for a clique of French poets); its application in France to new developments (especially to Mallarmé's poetry); and its spread to other countries. Wellek discusses the roles of such Anglo-American importers of the term and idea as George Moore, Edmund Gosse, Arthur Symons, James Huneker, T. S. Eliot, Ezra Pound, and Edmund Wilson. Many of Wellek's own assumptions about Symbolism derive from Wilson's *Axel's Castle* (1931). "In the United States

Wilson's reasonable and moderate plea for an international movement was soon displaced by attempts to make the whole of the
American literary tradition symbolist" (*Discriminations*, 101).
In Italy symbolist influence was small, in Spain central, in Germany
less complete than Symons assumed in his *Symbolist Movement in
Literature* (1899), in Russia dominant, in Czechoslovakia established, and in Poland accepted in practice but not in name.
These divergencies prompt Wellek to flirt with a few causal explanations regarding Germany, but he admits that the variables are
too great, the method too unsystematic, the speculations too easy.
Wellek expertly disposes of arguments which would preserve "Symbolism" for the Moréas group, for the French movement from Nerval
and Baudelaire to Claudel and Valéry, for all literature. He recommends "Symbolism" as another period term or "regulative idea"
like Renaissance, Classicism, Baroque, Romanticism, and Realism.
Symbolism refers to European literature roughly between 1885 and
1914 (between Realism/Naturalism and the new avant-garde movements), an international movement radiating first from France but
producing poets like Yeats, Eliot, Stevens, Hart Crane, Stefan
George, Rilke, Hofmannsthal, Blok, Ivanov, Bely, Darío, Machado,
Guillén; novelists like James, Joyce, Mann, Proust, Gide, Faulkner,
Lawrence; playwrights like Ibsen, Strindberg, Hauptmann, O'Neill;
and critics like Mallarmé, Valéry, Remy de Gourmont, Eliot, and
Yeats—the predecessors of many contemporary American and
French Symbolist interpreters.

Summing up his work on periodization, Wellek contributed
lengthy articles to the distinguished *Dictionary of the History of
Ideas* (1973) on "Periodization," "Classicism," "Baroque," "Romanticism," "Realism," "Symbol and Symbolism," as well as entries on
"Evolution" and on "Literature and Its Cognates."

VII *Language and Aesthetics*

Though less sanguine in recent years about the application of
linguistics to literary study, Wellek is not convinced, as was F. W.
Bateson, for example, that it is totally irrelevant. Wellek's response
to papers read at Indiana University in 1958, "Style in Literature,
Closing Statement," draws heavily on *Theory*.[29] He defines for literary criticism the limitations of anthropological description, psychological quantification, and linguistic phonics.

In his Bellagio paper "Stylistics, Poetics, and Criticism" (1970),

Wellek sharply distinguishes among the three disciplines. For him the discipline of stylistics is still part of linguistics. Systematic analysis of a work of art may widen into analysis of an author's total work, a genre, a period, a nation's art; many literary problems, however, go beyond particular verbal formulations, as the influential *Stilforschung* movement demonstrates. Stylistic analysis can support aesthetic explanation, but stylistic methods, particularly quantitative, cannot establish the ground of total evaluation.[30] For this, the literary critic cannot appeal to rhetorical categories or formalist intricacies. As Wellek many times has said, the critic must appeal "to extralinguistic and extrastylistic values, to harmony and coherence of a work of art, to its relation to reality, to its insight into its meaning, and hence to its social and generally human import" (*Discriminations*, 342).

Wellek wrote "Vernon Lee, Bernard Berenson, and Aesthetics" (1966) for a testimonial volume honoring the great Italian scholar Mario Praz, who agrees with Wellek's theory of literary history. This essay included in *Discriminations* is "marked by ease and graciousness," says one reviewer; Vernon Lee and Berenson "come across as humans," says another.[31] Wellek's little excursion into critical biography finely interweaves the story of their developments, their reputations—and their curious quarrel. Socialist, feminist, and pacifist, Vernon Lee (Violet Paget, 1856–1935) renewed and justified her early love of art in the late 1880s, after she discovered the theory of empathy, *Einfühling*. Possibly as early as 1891, she had met the young Bernard Berenson (1865–1959). "Some time in 1894 or 1895," writes Wellek, "an illumination came over Berenson: he discovered 'tactile values,' '*Einfühling*,' 'volume' as a criticism of painting" (173).

Like Vernon Lee, Berenson must have read Adolf Hildebrand's pamphlet *Das Problem der Form in der bildenden Kunst* (1893). Tenaciously, Wellek reconstructs Berenson's charges of plagiarism and Vernon Lee's defenses. Behind each lay Pater's and Emerson's views of art as mystical rapture; and behind each lay the German theorists from whom both sought scientific explanations for subjective reactions. Ironically, Vernon Lee's readers today value the charming essays praised by Mario Praz rather than her studies in empirical psychology; even more ironic, Berenson's growing fame rests less on his aborted theory and his art history than on his autobiographies and diaries.

No doubt Wellek's frequent references to Leo Spitzer's studies

in stylistics and semantics enhanced the fame of that Romance philologist. A *Privatdozent* at the University of Vienna when Wellek
was but a schoolboy, Spitzer later taught at other universities before
joining the Johns Hopkins faculty in 1936. In 1947, Wellek visited
Spitzer in Baltimore, met A. O. Lovejoy, and lectured at the History
of Ideas Club. Wellek's critical obituary—"Leo Spitzer (1887–1960)"—
honors him as the last of the great German philological quartet, as
the peer of Vossler, Curtius, and Auerbach. Wellek rectifies his
inadequate treatment of Spitzer in *Theory:* "By far the bulk of
Spitzer's writings and all his later work can be interpreted and
understood without recourse to the philological circle, intuition, or
depth psychology" (*Discriminations*, 200).

As one expects, Wellek zeroes in on Spitzer's development as a
literary theorist and critic. He approves of Spitzer's self-defining
polemics—also of his facts, categories, and insights into organistic
aesthetics. In spite of Spitzer's reservations about "narrow" American New Criticism, his concern with individual poems, close reading, and internal coherence is close to New Critical methods and
aims. From about 800 titles in Spitzer's writings, Wellek appends
a bibliography of thirty-four books and pamphlets, as well as a selected bibliography, eighty-eight items, of papers and reviews. One
should note also that Wellek wrote the appreciative introduction to
the Spitzer collection *Classical and Christian Ideas of World Harmony* (1963).

VIII   *Twentieth-Century Scenes*

In the *Concepts* essay "Main Trends of Twentieth-Century Criticism" (1961)—a foretaste of the last volumes of *History of Criticism*—Wellek observes that much criticism written today—
impressionistic appreciation, historical explanation, realistic comparison—is, of course, not new. His "Cook's Tour" points out salient
features and practitioners of contemporary criticism—Marxist, psy-
choanalytic, linguistic, stylistic, organistic formalist, myth, and existential. To be sure, Wellek is sympathetic to many insights of myth
criticism and existentialism. Still, he holds here to formalistic, organistic, symbolistic aesthetics. At the same time, he admits that
the New Criticism has reached a point of exhaustion. Criticism out
of the great German aesthetic tradition needs today, suggests Wellek, a closer collaboration with modern linguistics and stylistics, as

well as a clearer analysis of the stratification of the literary work of art.

What this essay does for the international scene "Philosophy and Postwar American Criticism" (1963) does, in part, for the national. Here Wellek interestingly gauges the allegiance of recent critics to major Western philosophers and philosophies. His survey adroitly identifies scores of direct and indirect descendants of such thinkers as Plato, Aristotle, St. Thomas, Kant, Schelling, Hegel, Herder, and Nietzsche. Wellek also takes up such currents as Marxism, Freudianism, and existentialism. In this unlimited expansion of criticism, Wellek hears a confusion of tongues, a new Tower of Babel.[32] Criticism once more seems to slide into something else—into sociology, politics, psychology, mysticism, or philosophy. That it will return to its *central* concern—interpreting literary art—is, of course, Wellek's hope.

Wellek's faithful junkets to Europe give him a sense of its bewildering critical atmosphere. "A Map of Contemporary Criticism in Europe" (1970)—in *Discriminations*—offered a bird's-eye view of the lay of the land as Wellek saw it in 1968. In England the antitheoreticians of the Leavis school are very active, but Wellek cited the work of recent philosophers and critics impressed by Wittgenstein's criticism of language. Theories and ideologies clash in France, with criticism tending away from the work of art in its integrity as it practices varieties of Marxism, psychoanalysis, and *"la critique de conscience."* In Germany Wellek found a variety of "close reading" reacting against *Geistesgeschichte*, with the left Hegelians (who appeal to Walter Benjamin) far stronger than the right. The Croceans are still strong in Italian universities, but Wellek discerned growing interest in Marxism, existentialism, and Spitzerian-Auerbachean methods. In Spain the "stylistics" of Dámaso Alonso stood out. The dogma of Socialist Realism still rules the Communist world, but the early Formalists attract some interest. Georg Lukács's two-volume *Äesthetik* (1963) is for Wellek a monument of the past.

In his uncollected short survey "American Criticism of the Last Ten Years" (1971),[33] Wellek admits that, in spite of his reservations, the criticism of the 1960s is no less diversified and exciting than the criticism of the 1940s. He comments on the survival of the New Criticism, the languishing activity of the Chicago Aristotelians, the expansion of myth criticism, the vigor of existentialism and the criticism of consciousness, the promise of the new linguistic meth-

ods, and the surprising absence of any Marxist criticism of consequence. A number of Wellek's cogent surveys of literary criticism
appear in important reference works: *Lexicon der Weltliteratur im
20. Jahrhundert* (1961), *Encyclopedia of World Literature in the
Twentieth Century* (1969, 1975), and *Enciclopedia del Novecento*
(1976), to name a few.[34]
     Perhaps one should note here that Wellek, as in his youth, still
delights in compendia. He has closely reviewed many important
research tools, among them, for example, *Handbuch der Weltliteratur*, *Dizionario Letterario Bompiani*, *Slavonic Encyclopedia*, and
the *Cambridge Bibliography of English Literature*. In the last-
named work, for example, he corrects plenteous errors—but with
good will and good wit: had John Bowles, for instance, been editor
of the 1736 edition of Skelton, "he'd have been only eleven years
old."[35]

IX   *Latter-Day* Critiques

     Characteristically, opinions in academic and general reviews of
Concepts of Criticism (1963) and *Discriminations: More Concepts
of Criticism* (1970) range widely. The vast majority, however, laud
the volumes for their brilliant scholarship, powerful arguments, and
essential unity. In his *Times Literary Supplement* feature review,
editor A. O. Aldridge recognized René Wellek as the world's leading
comparatist—and making the Kant-Wellek connection, described
the American's books as sometimes appearing as a "latter-day series
of *Critiques*."[36] Willard Thorp noted that in *Concepts* (edited by
Stephen G. Nichols, Jr., for Wellek's sixtieth birthday) the celebrated scholar had written his own festschrift, "a book, not a miscellany."[37] The independent essays, thought Alvin C. Kibel, "hang
together remarkably well."[38] Calvin S. Brown likened *Concepts*,
interestingly, to a painter's "retrospective exhibition."[39]
     "Into the dustiest corners of contemporary literary criticism,"
proclaimed G. N. G. Orsini, René Wellek "brings floods of light
and fresh air."[40] To his characterization of *Concepts* as learned,
acute, and instructive, E. N. Tigerstedt added that it provides
"God's plenty."[41] R. A. Sayce saw in *Discriminations* Wellek's "firm
attachment to the values of reason, his resistance to any form of
nonsense."[42] The same book, Emerson R. Marks noted, was "ad-
mirably named," that for Wellek terms have consequences: "they

clarify or obfuscate."[43] *Concepts,* said Ronald Hafter, "rigorously applies the principles it enunciates."[44]

Of course, Wellek's exhaustive delving—his factual and speculative density—is not everyone's cup of tea. There were those, like Allan Rodney, for example, who felt that the period essays especially were "smothered by the load of learning."[45] Edward Wasiolek, too, alluded to Wellek's "saturation scholarship," his "forbidding mesh of historical cross-references."[46] Again, J. D. O'Hara found a target: "Wellek goes as far back toward Genesis as possible and then tracks an idea doggedly through the ages."[47]

Some find Wellek's judgments overly cautious—not altogether indefensible in an historical critic, even if true. The melancholy *Choice* reviewer, no doubt disenchanted with criticism of criticism, longed for "less Polonius and more Hamlet."[48] Even Kibel, who recognized Wellek's coherence, succinct outlines, and intentions, claimed that in specific cases Wellek's arguments "evaporate in a mist of hesitations and qualifying phrases."[49] Though Wellek's mind, to Laurence Lerner, is lucid and well stocked, he found Wellek's method of surveying critical ideas and critical books less than exciting.[50] Wellek's "self-enclosure of scholarship," as Aldridge saw it, "unfortunately invites protest from those who feel left out."[51] To make *Discriminations* more acceptable to the general reader interested in literature, R. Gordon Cox advised thinking about it "in the first place as a work of reference."[52]

X   *Recent Papers*

Independently of papers for his *History,* René Wellek turns out essays and reviews. From time to time, usually on invitation, he ventures into related fields. Like "The Supposed Influence of Vico on England and Scotland in the Eighteenth Century" (1965),[53] "The Price of Progress in Eighteenth-Century Reflections on Literature" (1976)[54] reminds one of the method and erudition of *Kant in England.* His "Why Read E. T. A. Hoffmann?" (1967)[55] he has shortened as a foreword to Hoffmann's *Selected Writings* (1969). He has written a pamphlet for the 208-volume reprint series *English Criticism of the Eighteenth Century* (New York: Garland Press, 1969), as well as for the 101-volume *British Philosophers and Theologians of the Seventeenth and Eighteenth Centuries* (New York: Garland Press, 1975). Twice he has updated his penetrating survey "Coleridge: Philosophy and Criticism" for the Modern Language Association

88 RENÉ WELLEK

volume *The English Romantic Poets: A Review of Research and Criticism* (1950, 1956, 1972). Recently his old love for the Russian novel induced him to expand his "History of Dostoevsky Criticism" into a long paper on the "Russian Nineteenth-Century Novel," in essence a miniature history of criticism from Henry James to George Steiner.[56]

No Dr. Dryasdust, the polemical Wellek still speaks out in articles, reviews, and letters. Like his earlier "Some Principles of Criticism" (1963)[57] and his comment on a letter by the positivist Bernard C. Heyl in opposition to "Literary Theory, Criticism, and History" (1960),[58] such pieces as "Poetics, Interpretation, and Criticism" (1974), "Criticism as Evaluation" (1975),[59] and "Literature, Fiction, and Literariness" (1979)[60] continue to make plain his position. He rejects both the Marxist view which sees literature simply as a reflection of society and the structuralist view which sees language merely as a reflection of itself. Today the concept of "aesthetic" has been undermined, but Wellek says of the aesthetic function: "I hold to it tenaciously and defend it as a basic category of the life of the mind."[61]

His review of Robert Scholes's *Structuralism in Literature* (1974), for example, disapproves of Roland Barthes's semiotic *écriture*, of arbitrary and capricious interpretations, of the negation of interpretation, of the movement to make "structuralism" a religion.[62] In "The Attack on Literature" (1972), Wellek eloquently defends the great Western canon of literature; seeing the contemporary inability to judge quality as the "new barbarism," he argues vigorously and convincingly against the wholesale attack on literature by the political vandals, the distrusters of language, the cult of silence, and the electronic futurists.[63] Also, he rejects attempts to construct a disjointed history of paradigms modeled on Thomas Kuhn's *Structure of Scientific Revolutions* (1962), as when, for example, he himself is subsumed as a codifier under the paradigm "Tory Formalism" dominated by the "exemplar" T. S. Eliot.[64] But one would be mistaken to assume that René Wellek is not self-critical. His "Fall of Literary History" (1973) goes beyond his 1956 paper "The Concept of Evolution in Literary History." Tracing technical developments still seems feasible, but somewhat poignantly he ends one of his long-cherished illusions. He now accepts the view that literary art has no overall evolution: "I myself failed in *A History of Modern Criticism* to contrive a convincing scheme of development."[65]

Such directness and clarity have always been among Wellek's

qualities as a writer. With few exceptions, his later prose has been described as "lucid," "readable," "businesslike," "straightforward," "vigorous," "supple." Familiar with Wellek's "fluid drive" and Warren's "witty precision," W. K. Wimsatt correctly discerns that in *Theory of Literature* the sheer number and variety of systems and technicalities treated "on the run" were "no doubt a hazard to complete articulation and nicety of style."[66] Of key import to any critical style, of course, is tone. Nowhere in *Discriminations,* says Jacques Voisine, does Wellek lapse into the didactic.[67] Even Wellek's English censurer George Watson admits that "with fair though variable success" Wellek has solved the problem of tone—though to the metaphorical Denis Donoghue, Wellek "often speaks like the March of Time and occasionally like the Voice of Doom as he directs the weakest to the wall."[68] In his highly appreciative review of *A History of Modern Criticism,* Earl Rovit compared the "crabbed nervousness" of younger writers to the "magisterial grace" of writers like Perry Miller, Howard Mumford Jones, and René Wellek. "Their books," he said, "move at an unhurried, uncluttered pace."[69]

CHAPTER 5

History of Criticism *(I and II)*

WHEN Yale University Press published the first two volumes
of René Wellek's *A History of Modern Criticism: 1750–1950*
in 1955, John R. Willingham pointed out that scholars and librarians
have felt increasingly "hampered" by the lack of a definitive and
adequate survey of modern literary criticism.[1] The rapid expansion
of twentieth-century criticism and scholarship paved the way, of
course, for René Wellek's encyclopedic work. "No one," wrote M.
H. Abrams, "is better equipped than Professor Wellek with the
languages, the erudition, and the intrepidity needed for this formidable undertaking."[2] As *Booklist* early and accurately noted, it
is "the most ambitious project of its kind since George Saintsbury's
A History of Criticism and Taste in Europe appeared at the turn
of the century."[3] For the needed "clarifying, cartographic, signpost
effect on contemporary criticism," Newton Arvin was tempted to
feel, the first two remarkable volumes had come "in the nick of
time."[4]

The beauty of Wellek's *History* lies in its brilliant synthesis of the
general and particular from such a vast field of reference. The scholarship is immense, the quotations ample, the point of view clear.
While preserving "period" and "nation," Wellek surveys primarily
English, French, German, Italian, Russian, and American criticism—not in terms of *Geistesgeschichte* or Lovejoy's "unit ideas,"
but in terms of individual critics: the unique configuration of their
concepts, works, critical milieu, and contribution to modern critical
theory and practice. The method, as Lowry Nelson, Jr., points out,
allows for sympathetic and historical understanding, discussion of
texts, and balanced evaluation. "Of signal merit," he adds, "is Wellek's ability to explicate a critic's system or manner of thought."[5]
Indeed, disciples of the authoritative *Scrutiny* editor F. R. Leavis
still recall the extraordinary letter he received in 1937 from the

young Czech lecturer in London: "Allow me to sketch your ideal of poetry, your 'norm' with which you measure every poet."[6]

Still, more than one scrutinizer of critical works has declared that Wellek's systematic explications often fail to treat important texts as "wholes." Richard H. Fogle, for example, finds fault with Wellek for "breaking down critics into their identifiable concepts, without sufficiently noting the internal relationships which may represent a critic's true unity, coherence, and vitality."[7] But as Wellek later replied to Bernard Weinberg, another advocate of single-text analysis, "Critical texts are not works of art which, one could argue, must be analyzed and interpreted as totalities."[8] *Theory of Literature,* one recalls, distinguishes between literary art and literary study. Lee T. Lemon holds that, inevitably, Wellek's *History* reflects the unevenness of the diverse works he examines.[9] "Any particular chapter devoted to an individual or a small cohesive group," Ronald Hafter aptly notes, "invariably involves a complex of other figures, schools, movements, so that in structure the chapter resembles a waggon wheel with spokes gravitating outwards from the hub and leading to a wider referential circumference."[10]

Although Wellek focuses on individual genius, and in many cases on the totality of a major or minor critic's work as well as on single texts, a hallmark of his *History* indeed is his grouping of critics by doctrinal affiliation and his unifying effort to trace individual ideas backward and forward. He tells us, for example, that "Friedrich Schlegel introduced the term irony into modern literary discussion." Earlier one finds "only adumbrations in Hamann." Moving further back, Wellek notes that "Schlegel's use of the term differs from the earlier purely rhetorical meaning and from the view of tragic irony in Sophocles which was developed early in the 19th century by Connop Thirlwall." We then move back to Schlegel and slightly forward: "Schlegel's concept was taken up by Solger, in whom it first assumed a central position for critical theory and for whom all art becomes irony." Moving further forward, Wellek explains that Hegel and Kierkegaard misinterpreted Schlegel's irony as frivolous, wrongly identifying it with the Fichtean philosophy of the ego. While David Daiches, who thought that Wellek might be "too well qualified" to write the history of modern criticism, sees the technique as contributing to spatial and temporal continuity,[11] Fogle labels it "legalistic," leading Wellek into the "arid and tendentious discussion of sources."[12]

Originally, Wellek conceived of his *History of Modern Criticism:*

1750–1950 not in six volumes but in four. *The Later Eighteenth Century* (1955) and *The Romantic Age* (1955) were the first two volumes. But the third and fourth volumes (as well as the time spent in writing them) proved longer than Wellek had imagined. To *The Age of Transition* (1965) and *The Later Nineteenth Century* (1965), then, a later fifth volume, *The Twentieth Century*, would be added. Wellek's final manuscripts are so large, however, that Yale University Press has decided to divide it, the fifth volume to cover English and American criticism and the sixth Continental.

The solidity of Wellek's *magnum opus* is reflected in its imposing appearance and format. Printed on 1877 durable pages, the sturdy volumes (from the substantial first to the hefty fourth) connote distinction and permanence and have been referred to often as "monumental" and "magisterial." Though Wellek has rigorously screened and in many cases annotated his primary and secondary sources, his bibliographies and notes, as with all his books, impress us with their scholarly abundance. All quotations in the text are in English, but his thousands of endnotes include as a check the original French, German, Italian, and Russian. (For the sake of consistency and usefulness, even quotations from the criticism of Georg Brandes appear in the original Danish, though Wellek scrupulously points out in his bibliography that he had read Brandes only in German and English.) Attached to many chapters are more than a hundred notes. A. W. Schlegel, Coleridge, Taine, De Sanctis, and James— each receives over 200 notes, with Wellek bestowing on A. W. Schlegel a brave 241. Wellek's Chronological Table of Works—critical milestones discussed or mentioned in the text and listed under each country by publication date, author, and title—is indeed useful, as is his double index—one of names (analytical for major authors) and one of topics and terms.

Although, as Newton Arvin rightly notes, Wellek is "not committed to any simplistic, reductive, and illiberal conception of what criticism *ought* to be," to some impossible "pure objectivity,"[13] from the start Wellek announced his plan to write his history from a consistent point of view. "The history of criticism should not be a purely antiquarian subject but should, I believe, illuminate and interpret our present situation . . . comprehensible only in the light of a modern literary theory" (I, v). In his preface to the third edition (1962) of *Theory of Literature*, Wellek pointed out that his *History of Modern Criticism* "attempts to support the theoretical position here outlined as, in its turn, it draws criteria and values from *Theory of Literature"* (11). Thus the patterned flow of his history has a sense of direction: thesis (Neoclassicism), antithesis (Romanticism), synthesis (the Present). What for Wellek best illuminates and interprets the present historical concept of art qualified by the nonhistorical (our views, for example, on naturalism, art as expression, symbolic and mystical poetry) is the history of criticism which begins in the later eighteenth century, when the Neoclassical system of doctrines established since the Renaissance began to disintegrate. Historians like Croce and Huizinga support such a teleological method. R. S. Crane, Bernard Weinberg, and David Daiches reject it. In spite of this, some reviewers see Wellek's *History* as less a history than a vaguely connected collection of studies on individual critics.[14]

Volume I, *The Later Eighteenth Century,* begins with a penetrating background essay, "Neoclassicism and the New Trends of the Time." While recognizing the limitations of the Neoclassical doctrine, Wellek does not simply dismiss it, as so often happens from a Romantic point of view. He agrees with its aim to establish a poetics. Treating Voltaire, Diderot, and the lesser French critics first, Wellek next takes up Dr. Johnson and the host of minor but significant British critics. He follows this with a chapter dealing with the Italian critics. Exclusive of the background chapter, Wellek devotes about half the book to what Saintsbury slighted, the all-important German aesthetics and criticism of the time, chiefly represented by Lessing, Herder, Goethe, Kant, and Schiller. "The accounts," writes Robie Macauley, "in many cases masterpieces of compression and essence, are almost invariably both shrewd and generous."[15]

I French Criticism: From Voltaire to Rivarol

Less systematic than some of his contemporaries, Voltaire (François-Marie Arouet, 1694–1778) stands for Wellek as the best representative of late French Classicism. From Voltaire's numerous and far-ranging concrete pronouncements Wellek unfolds a coherent scheme, a taste for clarity, measure, and design firmly rooted in ancient Rome and seventeenth-century France. More aristocratically singular than rigidly Neoclassicist, however, Voltaire admired Vergil, Racine, Corneille, La Fontaine, and Molière; but during his stay in England (1726–28) his appreciations as set forth in *Letters Concerning the English Nation* (1733) increased.

Wellek explains, though, that as the "barbarous" Shakespeare more and more displaced French dramatists, Voltaire's brilliant satirical criticism "becomes much more sharp and even bitter and the acknowledgment of beauties less frequent and generous" (35).[16] Voltaire's argument against Shakespeare's "vulgarity," "improbability," and "indecorum" Wellek commends to our understanding and then refutes for our edification. Although he reads the *Essay upon Epic Poetry* (1727) less as historical criticism than as Voltaire's modernist defense of his own nationalistic *Henriade* (1728), Wellek is too cognizant of Voltaire's great poetic ambitions and minute critical attentions to agree with Saintsbury that this giant of the Enlightenment did not love literature.

Wellek's treatment of the baffling and dynamic Denis Diderot (1713–84) focuses on his naturalism modified by his sudden insights into the symbolism of poetry. Wellek discusses Diderot's rhetoric of sensations, his abortive theory of the metaphoric imagination, and his advocacy of bourgeois drama. Diderot's grasp of dramatic art became surer in *Le Paradoxe sur le comédien* (1778). Wellek also explains why Homer, Greek tragedy, Terence, Shakespeare, Richardson, and Racine impressed Diderot, while the speechifying clarity and lack of intensity in much Classical French drama depressed him. By attending to their polemical and generic contexts, Wellek discovers coherence and consistency in the contradictory variety of Diderot's views.

Most important, Wellek finds the common denominator—emotional effect—in Diderot's ambiguities. And Wellek traces a chronological shift in Diderot from naturalistic emotionalism to Neoclassical imitation—from the raw truth of nature to the finer truth of convention, from the actor carried away by emotion to the actor who imitates an interior model. "As we survey Diderot's critical work it is hard not to be unjust to the richness of its suggestions and the multitude of its interesting passages, ideas, and *aperçus*, because one cannot help seeing that Diderot is a man situated between two worlds, unable to choose between them" (61).

"Other French Critics" sums up the general trends of the divided eighteenth century. Hardly a literary critic in the strict sense, Jean-Jacques Rousseau (1712–78) is in Wellek's *History* because of his thrust toward the primitivistic view of poetry and the "conjectural" history of society. The Comte de Buffon (George Louis Le Clerc, 1707–88) has a niche because of his memorable *Discours sur le style* (1753), and Wellek correctly interprets Buffon's "the style is the man" as the Cartesian ideal rather than as expressed personality. A distinction is made between two influential Voltaireans: the loosely eclectic Jean-François Marmontel (1723–99), who wrote the two-volume *Poétique française* (1763), furnished the *Encyclopédie* with his contradictory literary theory, and tried, at least, to make literary history more scientific; and the liberal Neoclassicist Jean-François de la Harpe (1739–1803), whose sixteen-volume *Lycée* codified French taste.

Wellek finds unfortunate the influence of Diderot's early emotionalist theories on the colorless, German-born Friedrich Melchior Grimm (1723–1807) and on the more original Sébastien Mercier (1740–1807), who declaimed against all poetics and all system. Like the radical Grimm, the dogmatic sensualist the Abbé Condillac (1714–80), not exactly an *anti-philosophe,* also rejected fixed rules. Wellek finds novelty and freshness in the late eighteenth-century critics André Chénier (1762–94), who glimpsed an allegorical or symbolical conception of poetry, and Antoine Rivarol (1753–1801), who gropes in *De l'Homme intellectuel et moral* (1797) toward a new conception of the poetic mind.

II *English Criticism: From Johnson to Warton*

Samuel Johnson (1709–84) is for Wellek neither groping Preromanticist nor dogmatic Neoclassicist: he is "one of the first great critics who have almost ceased to understand the nature of art . . ." (79). "The observation," wrote Mark Schorer, "is as incontrovertible as it is startling."[17] Also thinking Wellek justified in charging Johnson with confounding art and life, Emerson R. Marks observes that "it is hard to imagine an indictment more destructive to the reputation of a literary critic."[18] Still, both Wellek and Marks show that within the limits of his Augustan taste Johnson wrote acute practical criticism, reconciling in his own mind the claims of realism, moralism, and abstractionism. Of historical importance is Johnson's acceptance of lifelike tragicomedy and his rejection of decorum and the unities of time and place, as well as his dislike of erotic, mythologic, allegoric, pastoral, and religious verse.

Indeed, the didactic editor of *Rambler* and *Idler,* attuned far more to English heroic pentameter than to aesthetics and cosmopolitanism, disfavored most blank verse and complex metaphoric poetry. Johnson's famous *Dictionary* (1755) and his great edition of *Shakespeare* (1765), however, helped awaken the English historical sense.

His biographical and critical *Lives of the English Poets* (1779–81) contains, as Wellek earlier noted in his *Rise of English Literary History*, an implicit scheme of poetic progress from the lowlands of *discordia concors* to the summit of Pope. Whatever "liberal" concessions Johnson made to the reader's taste, to the writer's genius, to different ages, places, and linguistic states, he offset by his appeals to durable esteem and universal common sense—to what Wellek sees, however, as the "very special" taste of abstract Neoclassicism.

In the bibliography to "Minor English and Scottish Critics," Wellek notes that "no part of our topic has been investigated more thoroughly and competently than this" (285). Again, Wellek draws on his *Rise of English Literary History* and "The Concept of Romanticism in Literary History." To unfold the story of the impressive aesthetics and historiography that helped destroy the position of Neoclassicism at home and abroad, Wellek treats a score of British critics and thinkers who prepared the way for the more radical Germans.

He reveals how discussions on beauty and on the poet reached an impasse, while those on the main problem of imitation (general versus particular) gave way to emotionalist theories about the effect of the imitated object. Older notions of ideal genres prevailed alongside assaults on the unities and defenses of Shakespeare's magnificent characters. Adeptly, Wellek analyzes answers to the question, Why do we derive pleasure from tragedy? In touching upon the shift in comedy from "oddity" to "sympathy," he points out the new regard for the "primitive" and "romantic," for the epics of Homer, Ossian, Ariosto, Tasso, and Spenser, and for the novel and lyric. Generalized feeling became personal emotion, "sincerity," confession. Wellek spells out the confusion that reigned concerning primitive societies and the progress or decline of poetry. All of this culminates, as earlier noted, in the antiquarian sterility of Thomas Warton's double view and its implications for today's all-embracing eclecticism.

III   *Italian Criticism: From Vico to Baretti*

Wellek sees the early eighteenth-century tradition of liberal Neoclassicism in Gian Vincenzo Gravina, Ludovico Antonio Muratori, and Pietro di Calepio. But it is of less influence on the second half of the century than that of English empiricism, French sensualism, and German Neoplatonism. Wellek takes pains to show the impact of the Neapolitan philosopher Giambattista Vico (1668–1744) and his *Scienza nuova* (1725) on Benedetto Croce and his *Estetica* (1902); in this highly critical section, Wellek concludes that Vico's radical insight into mythic truth and the poetic imagination had no effect on eighteenth-century aesthetics and criticism.[19]

Of minor critical importance were the notable poets Giuseppe Parini and Vittorio Alfieri—the first a sentimental moralist, the second an aristocratic free spirit. In several other critics Wellek traces the struggle between the old classicism and the new empiricism. In more detail, he discusses Melchiorre Cesarotti (1730–1808) and Giuseppe Baretti (1719–89), the latter best known in the English-speaking world for his *Dissertation upon Italian Poetry* (1753), *History of the Italian Tongue* (1757), and for his association with Dr. Johnson.

IV   German Criticism: From Baumgarten to Schiller

Wellek sees as the most important section in the first volume his discussions of the aesthetic and critical movement in Germany, for there a centuries-old struggle to achieve a proper theory of literature and art was culminated. To make the great flowering of German literary theory comprehensible, Wellek begins "Lessing and His Precursors" with cogent historical and analytical sketches. Wellek makes clear how the Leibnizian philosopher Alexander Gottlieb Baumgarten (1714–62) invented the term "aesthetics" but unfortunately lost his insight into aesthetic value. The clumsy writer Johann Elias Schlegel (1719–49), however, kept philosophy, art, and reality properly separated. The ideas of Baumgarten and Schlegel and those of empirical aesthetics and historicism (introduced into Germany by the Swiss intermediary Johann Jakob Bodmer, 1698–1783) combined in Moses Mendelssohn (1729–86). To these precursors, Wellek adds the Neoplatonic aesthetician Joachim Winkelmann (1717–68), who strongly influenced the younger literary critics with his ecstatic style and exaltation of the Greeks; in his *magnum opus, A History of Ancient Art* (1764), Winkelmann "not only describes and evokes individual works, not only tries to account by historical conditions for the unique greatness of Greek art, but quite consciously attempts to write an internal evolutionary history of style" (150).

Though Gotthold Ephraim Lessing (1729–81) holds a high place in German literature and in European criticism, Wellek finds his unsystematic theory and concrete criticism of English and Continental literature wanting. To be sure, Lessing scored dramaturgical victories over French Neoclassicism and raised the general level of German criticism, but his essays lack judgmental delicacy and scrutiny of masterworks. Wellek appreciates Lessing's knowledge of Sophocles, Terence, minor plays, English aesthetics and criticism. He finds his laudatory passages on Shakespeare, however, mostly derivative and hyperbolic. At times, Lessing's style is clear and sober, at times crude or pedantic.

Central to Wellek's discussion is his close examination of *Laocoon* (1766) and its relation to Lessing's *Hamburg Dramaturgy* (1767–69). That spatial and temporal arts differ importantly, that sheer pictorial detail is no guarantee of poetic unity, and that the prevailing stress on the visual is excessive—these ideas Wellek considers essentially sound. He accounts for Lessing's choice of drama as the highest literature, but remains himself unconvinced—as he remains unconvinced of Lessing's narrow Winkelmannian view that the fine arts represent only physical beauty, that the *Laocoon* statue, for example, expresses heroic composure rather than violent pain. Unfortunately, Lessing did not transfer to all art his insight into the value of coherence in tragedy; in fact, he reduced even tragedy to "an object lesson in humanitarianism" (174), interpreting Aristotle's catharsis in ethical terms. Like Johnson and Diderot, Lessing paved the way for nineteenth-century theories of psychological and social realism.

But Wellek shows that Lessing's restatement of French Neoclassicism proved unacceptable in Germany. Wellek's "Storm and Stress, and Herder" opens with a short description of the turbulent 1770s. He sketches the fervid introduction into Germany of English Preromantic aesthetics and Nordic poetry by the eclectic Heinrich Wilhelm Gerstenberg (1737–1823). Usually regarded as Herder's spiritual father, Johann Georg Hamann (1730–88) preached poetic genius and primitive myth; an aphoristic religious prophet, he rejected not only the Enlightenment, but modern civilization as well. To these, Wellek adds the influence on Herder of Winkelmann, Lessing, Vico, the British primitivists, and the French sentimentalists.

In turn, the radical views and the rhapsodic style of Johann Gottfried Herder (1744–1803) had an enormous impact on Goethe, Jean Paul, and the Schlegels. Wellek sees Herder as a great synthesizer, as the first critic who broke completely with Neoclassical rationalism, as the "fountainhead" of universal literary history. Aesthetics for Herder is sensualistic. Poetry is the art of the imagination, of emotion, expression, energy—the folk art of Ossian and Shakespeare. Criticism, in search of a poem's milieu, is empathetic and intuitive. While recognizing the enormous importance of the new historicism, Wellek sees its dangers in Herder's work as leading to complete relativism. On the one hand, Wellek indicates that Herder's conception of criticism is "too indulgent toward the purely naive, the mere lyrical cry, the merely spontaneous, and too inimical to great art, which may be intellectual, sophisticated, ironical, grotesque"; on the other, Wellek points out that "Herder was struck with the novelty of his discoveries, which were fresh and appealing against the background of a decaying Neoclassicism, while we are inured to many romantic charms by a century and a half of their vulgarization" (195). Herder's arguments are fragmentary, his style is reckless, and his impressions germinal. Still, Wellek finds the inner cohesion of Herder's *Kritisches Wäldchen* (1769) impressive; Herder's conception of poetry (metaphoric, symbolic, mythic) sound; and Herder's ideal of universal literary history (based only on his sketches, outlines, and questions) clear.

By seeing Johann Wolfgang von Goethe (1749–1832) as an "important link in the chain of German speculation on art and literature" (255), Wellek strikes a balance between Sainte-Beuve's "extravagant admiration" and Saintsbury's "irritated depreciation." Accounting at this time for the failure of scholarship to provide a definitive volume on Goethe's scattered literary criticism, Wellek suggests sources and a method for such a volume. Here he simply discusses Goethe's criticism before and after the Italian journey. To Herder's pupil in search of beauties, aesthetics meant little: the histrionic Sterne is a model of sincerity, Ossian expels Homer in Werther's heart, and forgotten for the melancholy Hamlet is "the active Hamlet who talks bawdy and daggers, kills Polonius like a rat, and sends Rosenkranz and Gildenstern to their death . . ." (205).

Goethe became an important critic only after his return to Classicism, but many of his dualities (allegory-symbol, Romantic-Classic, organic-inorganic) seem to Wellek obscurely formulated. Goethe's four-volume autobiography, *Dichtung und Wahrheit* (1811–33), falls short of its self-analytical aim. Though Wellek agrees with Goethe's insight into Byron's deficiencies, the late delicately balanced criticism of meditation is generally disappointing, for it led to good intentions and critical relativism. Particularly disturbing to Wellek, of course, is Goethe's identity of art with nature: "It is inconceivable that an ideal existence can follow the same laws as a natural being and that, in practice, the artist or critic can ever discover this presumed identity" (226).

In the last chapter of *The Later Eighteenth Century*, "Kant and Schiller," Wellek elucidates Kant's *Critique of Judgment* (1790), the book which, like the early *Critique of Pure Reason* and *Critique of Practical Reason*, created a surge of interest in aesthetics and poetics—and, one might add, new difficulties of comprehension, particularly for English readers. As one expects, Wellek defends the philosopher's systematic isolation of the aesthetic realm from the realms of science, morality, and utility. Although Kant hesitated to apply explicitly to art his influential theory of the sublime (reason and imagination in conflict), Wellek insists that Kant did not deny art's enormous role in society and metaphysics.

Wellek touches upon key ideas in Kant, but stresses the philosopher's view of the aesthetic state—the proper attitude toward the work of art—as one of "disinterested satisfaction" *(interesseloses Wohlgefallen)*. Kant rejects a priori principles, laws, and rules of criticism, but indicates how subjective aesthetic judgment claims universality by appealing to a common human sense, to an ideal totality of judges, to a criterion neither altogether relative nor absolute. Wellek notes that Kant, as a reader of German, French, and English literature, also speculated on the nature of literary criticism as concrete, historical, individual, comparative, and introspective. His practical criticism, however, is limited and undistinguished.

This brief treatment of Kant Wellek later developed into his "masterly"[20] essay in *Discriminations*, "Immanuel Kant's Aesthetics and Criticism" (1970). Again concentrating on Kant's influential motifs and solutions rather than on his elaborate scholastic divisions and argumentation, Wellek clarifies further the questions of autonomy, criticism, mediation, organicity, reconciliation of the particular and the general via the "Idea" ("Symbol"), and the character of the sublime—particularly in its application to tragedy (spiritual triumph over physical defeat) by Schiller and A. W. Schlegel. Viewing the thought of Kant and the Kantians as still vital in a world of extreme relativism, Wellek thinks that even Kant leaves too much in the realm of the subjective, not enough in the realm of objective art structures. The unphilosophic English reviewer Laurence Lerner found this treatment of Kant "extremely useful," for it would save busy people from reading Kant![21]

For Wellek, the Kantian Friedrich Schiller (1759–1805) "sums up and salvages the heritage of the 18th century and yet is the wellspring of romantic criticism which spread from Germany, mainly through the influence of the elder Schlegel, throughout Europe" (255). Wellek's sympathetic account shows how the poet-playwright Schiller—holding to such Neoclassical insights as impersonality, objectivity, and the eternal principles of nature—recognized in his *Letters on the Aesthetic Education of Man* (1795) the separate aesthetic realm and its relation to morality and civilization. Avoiding mysticism, Schiller tried to abandon external genre classification for a theory of four modes of feeling which, though puristic, "moves in the right direction" (254).

Wellek observes, however, that Schiller's stress on the general, the universal, and the conventional at times divorced him from concrete reality, making, for example, his "progressive" philosophy of history (the reconciliation of man and nature), seem utopian. This is not the case, however, with another work Wellek reads closely, *On Naïve and Sentimental Poetry* (1795–96), a reformulation of the old Ancient-Modern debate: the unified naive feelings as opposed to the divided sentimental feelings. Wellek lists a number of figures, past and present, upon whom Schiller's ideas—ignored for the most part by Saintsbury—made a powerful impact.

The gradual shift from a theory of imitation to a theory of expression is completed in *The Romantic Age*. Volume II begins with the Brothers Schlegel (whom Wellek exalts to the central position in the history of modern criticism) and with clarifying expositions on difficult and little-known German aestheticians and critics. But before his big chapters on Wordsworth and Coleridge, Wellek, with some unusual stresses, treats a half-dozen minor British critics. Each metaphorical critic—Hazlitt, Lamb, Keats—discovered something in Coleridge's eclecticism. *The Romantic Age* then provides highly discriminating accounts of Madame de Staël and Chauteaubriand, Stendhal and Hugo. After emphasizing certain motifs in Italians like Foscolo, Manzoni, and Leopardi, Wellek returns to a number of Germans, concluding with Schopenhauer and, finally, Hegel. Throughout, as Wellek steers his "middle course" between aesthetics and impressionism, he tries to locate anticipations of later views, to bring Romantic critics into close relationship with modern trends, though contemporaries, of course, often ignore or condemn their Romantic predecessors.

V German Criticism: From the Schlegels to Jean Paul

Wellek devotes his first two chapters to the Brothers Schlegel, writers of the review *Das Athenäeum* (1798-1800) and formulators of the famous, still pertinent, theory of Romantic criticism. Even in Germany these chapters were recognized as novel in their emphasis. Wellek details the three critical periods of the younger, more original Friedrich (1772–1829), whose early distinction between Classic and Romantic modified Schiller's theory of the "naive" and the sentimental. "What was needed," Wellek indicates, "was only to change the minus signs into plus signs in front of the characterization of the moderns" (12).[22] In his compact Platonic dialogue *Gespräch über die Poesie* (1800), Schlegel demanded a new myth: elaborate, philosophical, symbolical, ironical—ironical in high detachment, not in auctorial interference. Its all-embracing genre was the "impure" novel, the *Roman*.

Wellek elucidates Schlegel's distinction between *exclamatory* criticism which stimulates literature and *explanatory* criticism which must not practice Herderian tolerance. But intuition, close attention, reconstruction, and characterization of the work of art and the author's psychology in relation to the history of art, criticism must assign value and nonvalue to the work of art. Wellek acknowledges Friedrich Schlegel's contributions to hermeneutics, Indic studies, and, of course, to the criticism of Greek poetry, the Nordic Middle Ages, the Renaissance, and modern German literature. Still, he contends that, in spite of occasional pretentiousness and triviality, Schlegel's thought on irony, myth, the novel, and criticism alone makes him "one of the greatest critics of history" (35).

Like the incitant Friedrich, the restrained August Wilhelm Schlegel (1767–1845) was influenced by the Herderian ideal of world literature and the Schellingian *Naturphilosophie,* and he, too, wrote wide-ranging criticism and literary history. August Wilhelm's popular Vienna lectures, *Dramatic Art and Literature* (1809–11), account, in large part, for his greater effectiveness in and out of Germany. While showing the striking agreement between the brothers and the "general sanity" of their position, Wellek also reveals important differences of emphasis, tone, and personal development. August Wilhelm's more crafted criticism is technically

closer to the "inexhaustible" text than his brother's. His final theoretical formulations are more clear and systematic—as, for example, the famous Classical-Romantic contrasts: mechanical-organic,
plastic-picturesque, finite-infinite, closed-progressive, pure-mixed,
simple-complex, pagan-Christian, fate-character.

More than his brother, August Wilhelm is interested in original
language, "organic" structure, symbolism, and drama. Though Wellek thinks that A. W. Schlegel pushes his organism metaphor (poem
as animal) too far and the inspiration-consciousness problem not far
enough, the elder brother is "remarkably conscious of the cooperation and interpretation of criticism and history, theory and practice"
(54). Through art history and theory—between historicism and absolutism—subjective criticism locates objectivity, a point of view
best exemplified today, one might add, by Wellek's mediating "Perspectivism."

The work of F. W. J. Schelling (1775–1854) on idealism made a
great impact on the German Romantics, Coleridge, Emerson, and
others. Schelling's central lectures, "Philosophy of Art" (1859), were
published posthumously. "While Kant was at great pains to distinguish between the good, the true, and the beautiful, Schelling enthrones beauty as the highest value" (74). Art, the link between
finite and infinite, competes with nature's creative power. But for
Wellek, Schelling's claims for beauty are grandiose, his philosophy-
art relationship shifting, his notions on forms often fanciful and
confusing. Schelling's genre theory comparing lyric to music, epic
to painting, drama to sculpture, and novel to chivalric romance is
ingenious, and his view of *The Divine Comedy* as an epic *sui generis*
is perceptive—as is his idea of tragedy as free character in a fixed
world, comedy as fixed character in a free world, and modern tragedy as a mix.

The theory of Novalis (Friedrich von Hardenburg, 1772–1801) is
essentially "mysticalized Schelling," and his criticism is "aphoristic
grace." Saintsbury's claim that Novalis is Germany's greatest critic
is extravagant. Interesting to Wellek is Novalis's confession of an
imperfect understanding of Shakespeare and his reading of Goethe's
Wilhelm Meister as an anti-Romantic novel, claiming as *the* Romantic
novel his own unfinished *Heinrich von Ofterdingen*. Exalting the
poet-priest and the novelist-*Romantiker*, Novalis sees poetry as
magic and metamorphosis, religion and philosophy, free association
and play, fairy tale and dream, chance and Aeolian music, symbol
and truth. His criticism seems to Wellek "a strategy of finding the

place of a work of art, discovering its proper readers, defining its position in the world of poetry" (87).

The work of Wilhelm Heinrich Wackenroder (1773–98), "hardly a *literary* critic," is for Wellek too important and novel to be ignored. Deriving from Hamann and Herder, Wackenroder saw art as revelation, as a godly hieroglyphics. Since inspired works cannot be compared, he recommended not criticism, but universal toleration. Wellek captures the "desperate sound" of the last chapters of *Phantasien über die Kunst* (1799). Shortly before his death, Wackenroder wondered whether the source of feeling is metaphysical or physical, whether art is religious truth or a stay against time's relentless wheel.

Beginning with his friend Wackenroder, the eclectic Ludwig Tieck (1773–1853) reflects contemporary aesthetic theories and importantly speaks of the Romantic artist. But because Tieck's arguments are loose and lean, Wellek ranks this leader of the Romantic school—a title which Tieck later resented—below the Schlegels. He often fails as a critic of Shakespeare and is a mediocre but erudite student of the Spanish Golden Age. Wellek recognizes his contributions to the revival of Old German literature, his pronouncements on almost every writer of world literature, his editions of German writers, and his criticism of Goethe.

More difficult to define is the position of the novelist Jean Paul (Johann Paul Richter, 1763–1825). His florid *Introduction to Aesthetics* (1804) is for Wellek witty but sane. Great art for Jean Paul neither copies nor annihilates the world—it deciphers it: the self-conscious poetic genius dreams voluntarily, manipulates language, creates a second world out of the pandemonium of his own humanity. Thus Jean Paul's Romantic view of medieval Christianity and ancient Greece grew, embracing Nordic, Indic, and Near Eastern Romanticism. Jean Paul's stress on the novel—on character as individual and universal, physical and mental—defends his own practice. Most ingenious to Wellek is Jean Paul's thought on wit, humor, and the comic—thoughts which influenced F. T. Vischer, Coleridge, and George Meredith. His distinctions between psychology and poetics, however, are fuzzy. Wellek characterizes Jean Paul's practical criticism, mostly on German writers, as shrewd but impressionistic, as insufficiently analytical.

VI *English Criticism: From Jeffrey to Keats*

Wellek's essay on "The Concept of Romanticism in English Literary History" assists his chapter on minor English critics. Though English writers did not use the terms "Romantic," "Romanticist," and "Romanticism," they clearly knew that a European movement rejecting eighteenth-century poetics and practice was afoot. Wellek devotes about half the chapter to exposing the motley Neoclassical-Romantic theory behind the contradictions of the decorous and nationalistic *Edinburgh Review* critic Francis Jeffrey (1773–1850). A sentimental prude, he is remembered today mainly for his sallies on Wordsworth's poetry of "private" associations.

Unlike Jeffrey, *Quarterly Review* nationalist Robert Southey (1774–1843) was less a critic than a moralist, antiquary, and literary historian. Wellek also finds undistinguished the criticism of the undiscriminating antiquary Sir Walter Scott (1771–1832). Again, the tolerant critical (not political) spirit of the time pervades the art-minded *Essay On English Poetry* (1819) by Thomas Campbell (1777–1844). Wellek merely glances at the erratic Lord Byron (George Gordon, 1788–1844), at his emotional confession of poetic errors and his puerile defense of Pope. Unlike Byron, the Platonic Percy Bysshe Shelley preserved his faith in the truth of the imagination. Wellek finely criticizes Shelley's volcanic answer—the famous *Defense of Poetry* (1821)—to Thomas Love Peacock's cynically humorous "Four Ages of Poetry" (1820). Praising Shelley's historical insights, Wellek reproaches him for his self-defeating view of poetry as inspired vision rather than as deliberate art. That poetry is part of the fabric of society and the process of history—in this, Wellek concludes, is the real influence and truth of Shelley's defense.

Although William Wordsworth (1770–1850) is usually considered the manifesto critic of English Romanticism, Wellek finds his role in the history of criticism "ambiguous and transitional" (149), his small body of criticism "rich in survivals, suggestions, anticipations, and personal insights" (150). Wellek accentuates Wordsworth's theories as independent of those of Coleridge. The Prefaces of 1800 and 1815, the Appendix of 1802, the Supplementary Essay of 1815, the three essays on epitaphs, and the correspondence—these make up the sparse criticism from which Wellek extracts "the peculiar and valuable" (150). He traces Wordsworth's disdain for poetic diction to the poet's emotional-intellectual development, his regard for truth and accuracy. But Wordsworth's experimental call for "natural language" is not central. Wordsworth desires not a low but a common language, one as passionate and heroic (if figurative) as the language of Thomas Gray's bards. He was affected by the intricacies

of Spenser, Milton, and selected Augustans, as well as by simple
poetry.

The criterion of sincerity, as Wellek always insists, is a poor test
for literary worth. Wordsworth came to understand that not the
original emotion, but a "kindred" one, is the right one for poetry.
But justifying metric pleasure by its "good" effect inclines to propaganda and didacticism, to judgment by proper intention and subject
matter—as later in Tolstoy. Wordsworth's view of the imagination
vacillates, but Wellek sees no confusion between poetry and religion; both oppose science. Clarence D. Thorpe's claim that Wordsworth and Coleridge deeply disagreed about the fancy-imagination
distinction is not convincing. Wellek finds unfortunate Wordsworth's rare employment of his insight into the poem as a "wholeness."

As in *Kant in England* and elsewhere, Wellek acknowledges the
great importance of Samuel Taylor Coleridge (1772–1834) as a mediator between the German idealists and the British empiricists.
But Wellek still ranks him as philosopher and critic much lower
than have Saintsbury, Symons, Muirhead, Richards, Read, Abrams,
and many others. Richard H. Fogle humorously comments that "to
talk about Coleridge you have first to find some way of getting
around Wellek."[23] Try as he will, Wellek simply cannot absolve
Coleridge of his enormous debt to Kant, Schiller, Schelling, the
Schlegels, and Jean Paul. Coleridge's dependence on their ideas
and terminology does not mean that he merely parroted them.
Certainly his desire for system and unity—for an epistemology and
metaphysics underlying his aesthetics, literary theory, and critical
principles—differs from previous English writers. Mark Schorer has
observed that Wellek's precise definition of Coleridge's limitations
reveals "the seminal sources of Coleridge's continuing powers."[24]

In abundant detail, Wellek elucidates Coleridge's theory of literature in *Biographia Literaria* and in other works, especially his
ideas on the equipment of the poet (often confused with poetry
itself), on the imagination over the fancy, and the reason over the
senses. Of course, Wellek approves of Coleridge's speaking of poetry
in terms of wholeness, unity, and continuity. But he finds Coleridge's implied psychological criticism and his genre criticism disappointing. Coleridge's poetics and practical criticism are stronger
than the realm between: often his remarks on Shakespeare, Milton,
Cervantes, and Dante seem to Wellek trite or implausible. But
criticism of English and Continental contemporaries is shrewd and

sensitive. Almost all English critics to follow, Wellek concludes, found something useful in Coleridge's wide eclecticism. "His very looseness and incoherence, the wide gaps between his theory and his practice, his suggestiveness, his exploratory mind, his 'inquiring spirit'—these will always appeal to certain apparently permanent features of the Anglo-Saxon tradition" (187).

The roots of later English "impressionistic criticism" lie in the general shift of sensibility, but more clearly in the evocative, metaphorical, and reminiscent criticism of Charles Lamb (1795–1834), William Hazlitt (1788–1830), and John Keats (1795–1834). Lamb anticipates Hazlitt's methods, but falls short of the latter's wide range and theoretical awareness. Notwithstanding A. C. Bradley's and E. M. W. Tillyard's high praise for Lamb's elegant essays, Wellek finds the critical arguments in, say, the influential *Specimens of English Dramatic Poetry* (1808) generally weak. But Wellek credits Lamb's exquisite "marginalia" with the single point well taken and the new taste for the Baroque. In Lamb's exclamatory criticism, Wellek identifies what many readers still consider the only test of true poetry, "the criterion of the thrill down the spine, the bristling beard, the rise in the pit of the stomach . . ." (193).

While Wellek finds Lamb of marginal interest, he makes much of Hazlitt's metaphorical criticism, taste, and psychological framework. Lamb's prose, writes Hazlitt, "runs pure and clear, though it may often take an underground course, or be conveyed through old-fashioned conduit pipes" (196–97). At best, says Wellek, this method characterizes styles, describes characters, recalls scenes; at worst it gushes—and Wellek himself comes up with a waggish metaphor of Hazlitt's ideal critic serving as "an enthusiastic guide through a picture gallery, or as a host in a library who pulls out his books and points to favorite passages or recalls incidents and scenes in them and remembers when and where he read them" (197). Wellek importantly marks how the individualistic Hazlitt, journalistic middleman to a limited but growing middle class, tried to infect his readers with his gusto, with his myriad literary joys and bookish intimacies.

Wellek plays up Hazlitt's scepticism of critical abstractions and metaphysical wit. Still, Hazlitt held assorted notions on Wordsworthian particularity, the sympathetic imagination, objective passion, and the decline of imagination and individuality. Wellek judges Hazlitt's *Lectures on English Comic Writers* (1819) excellent; but his slightly earlier *Characters of Shakespeare's Plays* (1817) im-

108   RENÉ WELLEK

maturely confuses art and reality. Wellek recognizes Hazlitt's weak-
ness in the classical period, merit in the medieval, and strength in
the modern. Hazlitt tended to overrate poetic beauties, but Wellek
endorses his high opinion of Wordsworth, Coleridge, and Keats; his
moderate opinion of Shelley; his low opinion of Byron. Hazlitt was
too political to sanction pure aesthetics, yet Wellek commends Hazlitt's immediate effect: his lack of chauvinism, prudery, didacticism,
his efforts to give reasons, when possible, for his literary feelings.
    Wellek treats Keats as an "appendix" to Hazlitt, the critic whom
the poet most admired. Keats was neither original theorist nor
professional critic, but Wellek warmly says that "some of his scattered statements formulate his creed about the nature of the poet
and poetry so memorably that they ought to be recalled in any
history of criticism" (212). Wellek recalls the celebrated passages
in Keats's letters about the Shakespearean chameleon poet, his impersonality, his "negative capability," his capacity for sustaining
feelings of uncertainty and mystery, to *inform* himself into everything and into nothing. Speculating more about the nature of the
poet than the poem, the moody Keats late in his brief life admitted
to the realm of poetry the claim of humanity; Wellek nevertheless
insists that this belated recognition does not contradict Keats's earlier view of the poet as standing apart. Wellek quotes from "Ode
on a Grecian Urn" and chides T. S. Eliot for his confessed failure
to comprehend the Platonic "Beauty is Truth, Truth Beauty—."
Wellek explicates: "Art is perception of truth. Everything real (and
thus true) is beautiful" (215).

VII   *French Criticism: From De Staël to Hugo*

    The fall of Napoleonic Neoclassicism and the international ascen-
sion of *De l'Allemagne* (1813) by Madame de Staël (Germaine
Necker, 1766–1817) marked the turning point for Romanticism in
France. "But," Wellek cautions, "if we look at the French process
from the perspective of a general history of critical ideas, its significance will shrink considerably" (217). Before discussing the historical importance of Madame de Staël and François René, Vicomte
Chateaubriand (1768–1848), Wellek glances at Julien-Louis Geoffroy
(1743–1814), distinguished Empire critic, originator of the *feuille-
ton*, drama critic for the *Journal des débats*, a man who "calls for
the police to punish bad authors" (218). Still, his "firm hold on the

absolutes did not preclude a recognition of the actual historical variety of literature and an insight into its social conditions" (219).

Madame de Staël, like the English Preromantics, has a double view, one which jumbles an emotionalist theory with a creed of progress. Wellek spells out what makes *De la Littérature* (1800) often shadowy and mistaken. The superior *De l'Allemagne* (suppressed in 1810) characterizes the social, psychological, literary, idyllic Germany of Madame de Staël's travels. Wellek names her many informants and acknowledges her Schlegelian echoes, but decides that her French emotionalist conception remains intact: Madame de Staël is no propagandist for German symbolism or mysticism. Schiller's eloquence, Goethe's aloofness, Jean Paul's provincialism—these and other criticisms are in the main first hand.

Because of their common taste for French Classicism, Ossianic melancholy, and Rousseauistic yearning, the critical contrast between the Protestant Germaine de Staël and the Catholic Chateaubriand is less violent, says Wellek, than one might expect. Rhetorically contrasting passages from Classical and Christian literature, Chateaubriand directed his *Génie du Christianisme* (1802) toward Christian meditation and aesthetics, away from eighteenth-century scepticism and atheism. Wellek points up Chateaubriand's insight into a variety of French writers; into the Christianity of Baroque literature; into exotic nature and Gothic solitude; into cadenced description; into the kinship of literature, religion, and sensibility.

Wellek quotes from Chateaubriand's well-known essay on Dussault (1819), in which he advises foregoing the easy criticism of faults for the difficult criticism of beauties. With the exception of his concept of aesthetic personalism, "clichés of classicism" dominate Chateaubriand's pronouncements—whether in his early disparagement of Shakespeare, in defense of his own Christian epic prose romance *Les Martyrs* (1809), or in his late disdain for the younger Romantics. The digressive *Essai sur la littérature anglaise* (1836) is largely a grotesque compilation. Wellek closes with a blast: "The excesses of romantic aestheticism, its all-inclusive and therefore indefensible claims to the supremacy of art, of which Chateaubriand was one of the first proponents, have contributed to a reaction which has almost destroyed the legitimate position of literature and the arts in any scheme of human civilization" (239–40).

Before treating Stendhal and Hugo, Wellek sketches the growth of French Romanticism. The critical debate was narrow and simple: technically, the lyric was to become freer and the drama liberated

110

from the unities. Wellek sees this "tempest in an inkpot" as constituting no radical break with Neoclassical rhetoric until the advent of Baudelaire and Rimbaud. At the time, only the somewhat precious aphorist Joseph Joubert (1754–1824) understood the imaginative conception of poetry. Wellek explains that "the problem of the symbol in art is glimpsed without the term; the synthesis of the particular and the universal, the task of rendering in material language what is mental and spiritual" (243). Some of Joubert's formulations impress Wellek, not so his conventional views on Racine, La Fontaine, Corneille, and others.

Quite original is Wellek's stress on the often contradictory position of Stendhal (Henri Beyle, 1783–1842) in relation to Enlightenment, Romanticism, and Realism. Neither an aesthetician nor a theorist of consequence, the witty Stendhal nevertheless appears to Wellek as an engaging critic, a forthright Epicurean who judges art by the pleasure it affords. Such hedonism spells trouble for criticism, but Wellek can appreciate Stendhal's norms of taste, frame of reference, and intelligence. Surveying the voluminous criticism written over a long period, Wellek suggests reasons for Stendhal's curious attitudes: the admiration for Dr. Johnson, Jeffrey, Hazlitt; the hard line with the German symbolists and mystics; the tenderness toward the Italian dialect poets.

In some detail, Wellek discusses the polemical *Racine et Shakespeare* (1823, 1825), early pamphlets which jeer at French-Academy verse drama and cheer for French prose on stage. Besides historical drama, Stendhal championed modern dramatic satire and the psychological novel; his classic *The Red and the Black* (1831) epigraphically defines the novel as "a mirror walking down a road," but Wellek attests that Stendhal himself balked at its implications of photographic naturalism. "By his instinct for clarity, his rationalism in philosophy, his irony, his distrust of sentimentalism, and his love for understatement Stendhal derives from the 18th century, in spite of all his attacks on the courtly forms of French classicism" (252).

Although he characterizes criticism by the apotheosized Victor Hugo (1802–85) as unsystematic, undiscriminating, and impatient, Wellek argues for its reinstatement. From Hugo's flamboyant rhetoric, Wellek isolates signal insights and brilliant formulas about the nature of poetry. Hugo's *Préface* to *Cromwell* (1827), the chief manifesto of the French Romantic debate, is in part based on Madame de Staël, Chateaubriand, and Stendhal. But Wellek argues that Hugo's rejection of the rules, genre distinctions, and levels of style includes also a scheme of literary history and a reinterpretation of poetry; more systematic parallels of these existed at the time only in Germany and in Coleridge. Wellek weighs the pros and cons of Hugo's conception of the three great ages of poetry and remarks on his arresting notions about the internal order of a work of art, the union of opposites, and the transformation of the ugly and grotesque into a higher synthesis.

Though Wellek characterizes *William Shakespeare* (1864), Hugo's later major criticism, as disconnected, ostentatious, and long winded, he discovers something fresh: ". . . Among all the welter of names, exhortations, declamations against stupid critics, persecutors of poets, and so on, there are a few pages which show a remarkable insight into a mythic concept of poetry and anticipate the Jungian view of literature as a creation of 'archetypal patterns' " (257). By cutting through Hugo's "grandiose confusion"—the upshot of his titanic will to a total synthesis of life and literature—Wellek preserves what in Hugo's criticism seems valuable. "Another ancestor," as Newton Arvin puts it, "is thus happily rescued from the mausoleum."[25]

VIII   *Italian Criticism: From Manzoni to Leopardi*

In treating the Italian Romantic Movement, Wellek defines Madame de Staël's influence, the impact of the periodical *Il Conciliatore* (1818–19), and the roles of several patriots, realists, and moralists. Wellek reviews *Del romanzo storico* (1845) and *Dell' invenzione* (1850) of Alessandro Manzoni (1785–1878), explaining the dilemma of the renowned author of the historical romance *The Betrothed* (1827). Unable to accept Goethe's solution that in art both imaginary *and* historical characters are ideal, Manzoni repudiated art in favor of history, proof for Wellek of the vital distinction between historical art and historical truth.

The poets Ugo Foscolo (1778–1827) and Giacomo Leopardi (1798–1837) paradoxically quarreled with Italian Romantic theories, yet fostered European Romantic doctrine and literature. Wellek approves of Foscolo's efforts to preserve the illusion and individuality of art by rejecting Manzoni's ideal-historical distinction and the Neoclassical genre distinctions. Though Foscolo knew and loved several languages and closely argued about "heroic" Dante and "decadent" Petrarch, Wellek characterizes most of Foscolo's academic and exile criticism as inert, bombastic, and incoherent.

More original and striking is the lonely Leopardi. In *Zibaldone* (Leopardi's commonplace books written in Neoclassical terminology and published late in the nineteenth century), Wellek pinpoints items advocating illusion, mythology, fantasy, childhood, nature, God, nostalgia, and—most emphatically—lyricism. Saddened by the decay of the modern imagination, Leopardi looks with favor neither on drama nor the novel, only upon Homer, Pindar, Anacreon, Vergil, Lucretius, Lucian, Dante, Petrarch, and Tasso—to him all *lyricists*. Wellek regrets the critic's lack of tolerance and curiosity, but not inconsistently Wellek defends the poet's right to bias and dogmatism.

IX   German Criticism: From Görres to Hegel

The younger German Romantics, says Wellek, "turned to the study of origins, the Teutonic past, folk songs, folk tales, legends, the *Nibelungen,* the *Edda,* and in general to everything they thought was indigenous, aboriginal, pristine, 'German, untouched by the blight of modern civilization, and thus contributory to a recovery of the nation" (279). Wellek points to *Die deutschen Volksbücher* (1807) by Joseph Görres (1776–1848) as both a new manifesto and an early migration-of-themes study centered on sixteenth-century German chapbooks. Görres's evocative, analogical, metaphorical criticism praised simple, grand, organic folk poetry over most art poetry. Wellek finds pretentious Görres's identification of natural poetry with Eastern mythology.

Like Görres, the brothers Jakob Grimm (1785–1863) and Wilhelm Grimm (1786–1859), the founders of Germanic philology and "Germanics," admired world folk poetry, distinguished between ancient unconscious natural poetry and modern conscious art poetry, and pushed the origins of the epic (self-composed, collective) so far into the past that it fused with myth and mystery. Wellek touches upon Jakob's crabbed style, his erstwhile influential theory of linguistic decay, his argument for the *Renard* stories as old epic remains, and his Germanic distaste for complex learned Western poetry. Wilhelm could appreciate "natural" and "national" art poetry more than Jakob.

Wellek points to the new group's many collections, notably the Grimms' *Kinder- und Hausmärchen* (1812–15) and Arnim and Brentano's folksong collection, *Des Knaben Wunderhorn* (1805–1808). The would-be folk poet Achim von Arnim (1781–1831) correctly perceived unconscious creation in new poetry, conscious creation in old, exceptions to folk anonymity, and imperfections in Homer and in the *Nibelungen*. Because Arnim abandoned what to Wellek are sound Schlegelian insights, however, the criticism lacks coherence. Wellek also finds basic irrationalism in the remarkable essay "Über das Marionettentheater" (1810) of the dramatist Heinrich von Kleist (1777–1811), defender of unconscious creation.

Only in the little-known Adam Müller (1779–1829) does Wellek discern among the group an important theorist and eloquent practical critic, his ideas close to those of the Schlegels, Schelling, and Novalis. Employing a "mediating" relativism, Müller relies on the dialectics of the reconciliation of opposites. Wellek finds extraordinary for the time Müller's reconciliation of Latin and Teutonic poetic ideals, as well as his defense of both medieval low comedy and French tragic drama. Müller the Catholic also admires German-Christian tragedy, particularly Kleist's *Amphitryon*. His conception of Shakespeare lacks unity, but Wellek detects original comments.

To clarify the position of Karl Wilhelm Ferdinand Solger (1780–1819), Wellek draws not only on Solger's main work, the obscure dialogue *Erwin* (1815), but also on his *Vorlesungen über Äesthetik* (1829), on his minor writings, and on his correspondence, especially with Tieck. With his philosophy of irony as central to all art, his dialectical union of opposites, and his emphasis on concrete beauty, he joins those critics, Wellek declares, "who favor a fundamentally symbolic view of art as imagination" (303). To these ideas Wellek links Solger's practical criticism, mainly on ancient tragedy, Shakespeare, and Calderon. Although he finds Solger's attack on A. W. Schlegel's neglect of irony unconvincing, Wellek smartly resurrects Solger because of the role of artistic "irony" today.

And although the system of Friedrich Schleiermacher (1768–1834) fails to assimilate contradictions, Wellek commends it also to our attention, for he astutely sees the great Lutheran theologian as *the* aesthetician of Romantic expressionism. Wellek bases his exposition of Schleiermacher's heterogeneous system (rediscovered by Croce) on the lectures on hermeneutics and on aesthetics, the latter having antecedents in Baumgarten and Herder. Unlike Solger, Schleiermacher sees art as continuous as daydreaming but more imaginatively productive than remembered associations. Wellek touches on Schleiermacher's blurring of genre distinctions and on his concept of "divination"—the part explains the whole as the whole explains the part—in terms of the unvicious circle, the hermeneutic circle, the "circle of understanding."

Late in the nineteenth century the aesthetics of Arthur Schopenhauer (1788–1860) assumed historical importance, for he carried Platonic ideas into a time when Schelling and Hegel had suffered obloquy. To make the aesthetics evident, Wellek outlines Schopenhauer's metaphysics in *The World as Will and Idea* (1819, 1844). Will, the evil essence of the world, objectifies itself in appearance and idea; by reversing the Will, by identifying with others in pity and asceticism, one overcomes evil. Through art, through the disinterested contemplation of ideas, one momentarily escapes the Will, achieves a painless state. To this end of Eastern negative happiness Schopenhauer explains various poetic devices, but Wellek sees Schopenhauer's inspired poet as an inferior philosopher. Wellek illustrates Schopenhauer's German Neoclassical taste and comments on his advocacy in *Parerga* (1851) of simple, clear prose. But Wellek explains Schopenhauer's influential theory of music as a copy of the Will and of the lyric as the form both of knowing and willing. Schopenhauer's view of tragedy as unjust suffering importantly counters the theodicy of Lessing and Schiller, Wellek asserts, but the great pessimist's view lacks balance, tragedy's compensatory transfiguration, or spiritual victory.

German thought on art culminates in the aesthetics of Georg Wilhelm Friedrich Hegel (1770–1831), one of the most influential thinkers in history. Wellek envisions him as a Janus head: "one side looking back into the past, yearning for the Greek ideal of serenity and ideal art, the complete fusion of form and content that he saw in Greek sculpture, in Homer and Sophocles; and the other side turned toward the future, looking with unconcern and even satisfaction at the death of art as a past stage of humanity" (333–34). Cutting through the redundancy, asperity, and pedagogic levity of the posthumous *Lectures on Aesthetics* (1835), Wellek takes up such things as Hegel's influential method, his view of history and the hierarchy of art, his equation of metaphor with allegory, and, of course, his observations on particular classic and Western literary works.

At the heart of what he calls Hegel's "anti-aesthetic," Wellek unveils a contradiction: Hegel defines the work of art as a self-enclosed totality, but his rationalism fosters a form-content split, the destruction of the "dialectical unity of the sensuous and the idea" (320). If poetry is judged in terms of content alone, then

literature once more becomes a stepping stone to religion and philosophy—to absolute spirit, to the idea, to truth. Wellek explains
the relationship between Hegel's dialectics of the spirit *(Geist)* and
his three-stage scheme of developing beauty in art: Symbolic (Oriental), Classic (Graeco-Roman), Romantic (Western Christian). Poetry, because close to thought, is the highest art; epic, lyric, and
drama develop in sequence. Hegel views dramatic poetry (a combination of epic and lyric) as the highest literature. Wellek avers
that Shakespeare's tragedy resists Hegel's theodicy and dialectic.
(Two antithetical moral forces collide and end in a synthesis of serene
reconciliation.) Since Wellek believes in the permanence of art, he
thinks of Hegel and his work "as a summit, an end—indeed a dead
end" (334).

Still, for the historian of criticism, Hegel's *History of Philosophy*
(1833–36) is pertinent today, as Wellek pointed out in Budapest in
his recent "Reflections on my *History of Modern Criticism*" (1977).
Wellek himself has accepted Hegel's introductory dictum that "the
history of a subject depends closely on the concept one has of the
subject." Like philosophy, criticism depends on diversity—and is
conceived as "an organically progressive totality, as a rational continuity."And as the study of the history of philosophy is really the
study of philosophy, so the study of the history of criticism is really
the study of criticism—and the newest criticism, like the newest
philosophy, is the result of all preceding ones. Thus for Hegel (and
Wellek) history and truth really have no past. By implication, Wellek
declares, the historian has obligations to judge, to decide which
ideas belong to the chain of development.[26]

Thus Murray Kreiger earlier perceived correctly that Wellek's
unique fitness for writing critical history "arises not only for the
unmatched competence of his knowledge of the field, but also from
his demonstrated interest in the philosophy and methods of history."[27] Besides praising Wellek's unprecedented historical knowledge and judicial courage, many eminent scholars—Northrop Frye,
Erich Auerbach, and Sir Herbert Read among them—exalted the
initial volumes of Wellek's *History* for their awesome range, masterly command of detail, and synoptic clarity.[28]

CHAPTER 6

History of Criticism *(III and IV)*

W HEN the third and fourth volumes of *A History of Modern Criticism* appeared a decade later, in 1965, acclaim for Wellek's achievement mounted. Critics sympathetic to his high enterprise of narrating the drama of criticism indicated that René Wellek's work more than fulfilled the promise of the first two volumes, by then in German, Italian, and Spanish translations. As usual, however, English empiricists suspicious of Wellekian theory dissented. Still, Alfred Owen Aldridge in the influential *Times Literary Supplement* reasserted: "Such a work, carried through in so scrupulous and tenacious a spirit, is a mark of civilization at its best."[1]

While many American and European reviewers recited the customary tales about Wellek's vast learning, deep patience, and catholic sympathies, the noted Irish critic Denis Donoghue insisted that "Mr. Wellek is a little hard, almost totalitarian, with his great fools."[2] Like Donoghue, F. W. J. Hemmings shortsightedly defended journeyman criticism by attacking Wellek's reliance on aestheticians, philosophers, and history to help explain the contemporary critical situation.[3] But Wellek's severest critic seems to be an American: Roger Sale, pointing to Wellek's "theoretical inflexibility," "atomistic method," "isms within and across boundaries of countries and disciplines," and merely "knowing much more than others," venomously concluded that "the genius of English literature and criticism is not congenial to a continental philosopher like Wellek."[4] But on the prevailing "hierarchy of interpretations" such sarcasms rank low.

Volume III, *The Age of Transition* (the publisher's title), begins with French criticism before 1850, background to Sainte-Beuve. Italian criticism from Scalvini to Tenca follows. Wellek next treats English critics—Carlyle, De Quincey, Hunt, Macaulay, J. S. Mill, Ruskin—and American—particularly Poe and Emerson. Then come a host of German critics from Grillparzer to Marx and Engels. *The Age of Transition* closes with Russian criticism, the focus on Belinsky.

I *French Criticism: From Barante to Sainte-Beuve*

To present Sainte-Beuve, Wellek astutely surveys for the first time an array of interesting French critics before 1850, those who "laid the foundation of French literary history, formulated a symbolist theory of poetry, demanded a literature in the service of humanity, and started the art-for-art's sake movement" (1).[5] He examines Prosper de Barante's (1782–1866) study of the influence of letters on society, François Guizot's (1787–1874) argument for the influence of society on literature, Charles Léonard Simonde de Sismondi's (1773–1842) literary history informed by German historicism, and the ground for a history of medieval literature laid by Claude Fauriel (1772–1844) and his pupil Jean-Jacques Ampère (1800–64). In the main, Wellek finds the academic studies of Abel François Villemain (1790–1870) dreary, likening his position to Thomas Warton's. The cosmopolitan Philarète Chasles (1798–1873) sympathizes with so many literatures and subjects that art dissolves into history.

When dust from the Classic-Romantic fray began to settle, the cantankerous journalist Gustave Planche (1808–57) reacted in favor of Classical "good sense," which in practice, remarks Wellek, "turns out to be a denial of imagination and poetry" (17). At the Sorbonne, the witty bourgeois literary historian Saint-Marc Giardin (1801–73) preached the moral and social dangers of modern literature. Another critic who resisted "decadent" Romantic literature was Désiré Nisard (1806–88), who tried in his unitary, four-volume *Histoire de la littérature française* (1844, 1849, 1861) to establish criticism as an exact science by setting up ideal norms. Wellek judges most of the literary history of Charles Magnin (1793–1862) important, although his moderate claims and casual expression dim his position, a combination of symbolic poetics and the new historicism.

Apparently new is Wellek's discovery of organistic views in the lectures of Alexandre Vinet (1797–1847) and in the *Revue encyclopédique* articles of Pierre Leroux (1797–1871). Vinet read nineteenth-century French literature in terms of German ideal aesthetics, and Leroux (the one real critic among the Utopians) combines a theory of social art and symbolism. In the writings of Saint-Simon

(1760–1825), literature plays a minor role, but Saint-Simonians promised artists a leading role under socialism, as did the sentimental Charles Fourier (1772–1837).

Wellek distinguishes the sensual aesthetics of Théophile Gautier (1811–72) from the abstractions of Victor Cousin (1792–1867) and the humanitarianism of Theodore Jouffroy (1796–1842). In the preface to his famous novel *Mademoiselle de Maupin* (1834), Gautier lashes at progress and the Utilitarians, lauds Beauty and Art for Art's sake. Likening Gautier's method to that of the English metaphorical critics, Wellek describes the Frenchman's pictorial fantasy as "an elaborate mannerism, a virtuoso indulgence" (31). But the jovial Bohemian encouraged young artists and defended Baudelaire. In such books as *Les Grotesques* (1844) and *Histoire du romantisme* (1872) he helped reinterpret French poetic history and defend decadence.

No chapter bearing upon sixty volumes of deft and variable criticism can be complete. Still, Wellek masterfully particularizes the achievement of the major critic Charles-Augustin Sainte-Beuve (1804–69)—his historicism, his essayistic charm, his convincing voice, his vast learning, his good sense—his *centrality*. Though he defends Sainte-Beuve, Wellek does not ignore the critic's limitations—his distaste for the baroque, the grotesque, the sublime, and his unliterary stress on biography, psychology, and social history. Though this author of 640 weekly essays—*Causeries du Lundi* (1849–61) and *Nouveaux Lundis* (1861–69)—professed no rigid critical system, Wellek reveals presuppositions of Saint-Beuve's Romantic, impressionistic, and judicial periods—his attack on Boileau, for example, in the first period, his recantation in the second, his praise in the third. Wellek denotes in the versatile, ever-curious Sainte-Beuve "a basic sceptical and sympathetic historicism, a taste that harks back to the classical tradition but wants it moderately liberalized, and an increasing preoccupation with the new naturalistic, 'scientific' methods of studying literature" (70).

Sainte-Beuve's late theory of psychological types ("families of the mind") was never, Wellek emphatically insists, a substitute for individuality, the human portrait, the problem of appearance and reality (man and mask), the moral question of "sincerity." Wellek asserts that Sainte-Beuve, knowing the difference between art and life, upheld a symbolic view of literature, though at times he mistakenly favored personality over achievement. Wellek highlights Sainte-Beuve's methods and views: in *Tableau de la poésie française*

au XVIe siècle (1828); in the triumphant five-volume "hybrid" history
of the Jansenists, *Port-Royal* (1840–59); in *Chateaubriand et son
groupe littéraire sous l'Empire* (1860); in *Étude sur Virgile* (1857);
and in the memorable essays "What Is a Classic?" (1850) and "Of
Tradition" (1858).

Wellek concludes with an extended clarification
of Sainte-Beuve's concrete opinions—his reverence for the ancients
and dislike of the Middle Ages, his reservations about French Renaissance poets and appreciation of the Neoclassicists, his early defense of the Romantics and his attitudes toward his contemporaries
and English literature.

II   Italian Criticism: From Scalvini to Tenca

In Italy during the 1830s and 1840s, Wellek reports in his ar-
duously researched chapter written in the Biblioteca Nazionale in
Florence in the fall of 1959, political literary criticism was extreme.
Little-known in his own time but now admired, Giovita Scalvini
(1791–1843) often echoes the Germans, but his fragmentary work
shows both a rare sensibility and a rare grasp of Romantic doctrines.
Like him, the ingenious Vincenzo Gioberti (1801–52) knows German
idealism, but his systematic *Del Bello* (1841) is a farrago: "Lambs
and lions, St. Thomas, Malebranche, Thomas Reid, Kant, Schelling,
Hegel, and Cousin lie down together" (75); Wellek accounts for the
influence of Gioberti's interpretation of Dante as an orthodox phi-
losopher-poet-priest and Gioberti's scheme of Italian literary history
in his jingoistic *Del Primato morale e civile degli Italiani* (1843). The
irritable, prolific, erudite Niccolò Tommaseo (1802–74) would have
the believing artist unite religion and poetry, as did Dante; outlining
Tommaseo's contributions to historicism, linguistics, and European
literary opinion, Wellek decides that, despite the fine feeling for
words, "Tommaseo's almost inquisitorial moralism paralyzes his insights and sensibility" (80).

For the always fervent and often perceptive Giuseppe Mazzini
(1805–72) the mission of criticism is to prepare the collective poetry
of the socially perfect future, a notion of Providence which colors
all his judgments. Wellek touches upon two influential liberal literary histories that followed—the historiographically declamatory
but soberly compiled *Storia delle belle lettere in Italia* (1845) by
Paolo Emiliani Giudici (1812–72) and the simplistically framed but
lusciously "pagan" *Lezioni di letteratura italiana* (1866–72) of Luigi
Settembrini (1813–77). By grasping both the nature of art and the

power of the historical spirit, Carlo Tenca (1816–83) tried to reconcile liberal and Catholic viewpoints, to harmonize intellects—but
not until almost twenty years later, decides Wellek, did the great
synthesizer Francesco De Sanctis gratify this demand.

III   English Criticism: From Hallam to Ruskin

The introduction to this section condenses much information
Wellek gathered at the Huntington Library for his "sequel" to *The
Rise of English Literary History*. Looking at the 1830s and 1840s
in England, Wellek concludes that the idea of a coherent literary
theory fades: literature becomes misunderstood. Utility, anti-intel-
lectualism, and natural shrewdness result in anarchic impressionism.
As theory waned, indiscriminating antiquarianism and history
waxed, and no book replaced Thomas Warton's *History of English
Poetry*. Among several interesting failures, J. P. Collier's well-in-
tentioned *History of English Dramatic Poetry up to the Time of
Shakespeare* (1831) hunts "too many hares at the same time" (91)
and Henry Hallam's introduction to the *Literature of Europe in the
15th, 16th, and 17th Centuries* (1838–39)—Wellek wrote an unri-
valed introduction to the 1970 reprint—is "little more than a well-
informed catalogue" (90).

Like Thomas Carlyle (1795–1881), Wellek sees Romanticism as
a unity, as largely a reaction against the Enlightenment. Only Carlyle, Wellek declares, imported the concept of a national literature
unified by a national mind, the concept of literary evolution, and
the whole ideal of narrative consecutive literary history" (91–92)—
ideas related, one recalls, to Wellek's earlier discussions in "Carlyle
and German Romanticism," *Kant in England*, and "Carlyle and the
Philosophy of History." Here Wellek criticizes Carlyle's interesting
German interpretations—his *Life of Schiller* (1825) and his miscellaneous pieces on Goethe, Jean Paul, Novalis, and E. T. A. Hoffmann. But only from 1827–32 did Carlyle assimilate monism.
Believing afterward in dualism, in the universal struggle between
Good and Evil, Carlyle satirized the ethics of such contemporaries
as Burns, Scott, Byron, Shelley, and Keats. On the one hand, Wellek
regrets Carlyle's negation of literary criticism, his shift from art to
fact, from German historicism and symbolism to biography, didacticism, moralism, and "sincerity"; on the other hand, Wellek, as
ever, sympathizes with the deep moral basis of Carlyle's forceful
personality, his rejection of anarchy and blind faith.

And predictably cool, as usual, is Wellek's account of the impish Thomas De Quincey (1785–1859), who could declare that Kant never read a book and that *Wilhelm Meister* is obscene. De Quincey's critical allegiance, Wellek shows, is to Wordsworth, not to Coleridge—to empirical psychology and emotionalism, with only occasional symbolic echoes. Of De Quincey's famous distinction between poetry (the literature of power) and science (the literature of knowledge), Wellek indicates that the first term (like the German *Dichtung*) embraces imaginative lyrical prose. Earlier, Herder and Hazlitt identified "power" with emotional impact; not only is the power = emotion formula vague in the unsystematic De Quincey, but knowledge, after all, *is* power.

As in his "De Quincey's Status in the History of Ideas" (1944), Wellek again takes issue with Sigmund K. Proctor's claim for De Quincey's originality. Wellek detects little relationship between De Quincey's derivative theory and his prolix practical criticism. And the historian-critic pronounces De Quincey's view of French and German literature inept. Analyzing the well-known "On the Knocking at the Gate in Macbeth" (1823), Wellek suggests a simpler explanation for the crucial effect—not the isolation of the criminal pair, but our sharing in the apprehension and terror. Wellek implies—so Donoghue cracks—that De Quincey should have taken a few decent courses at Yale.[6]

Unlike De Quincey, the impressionistic Leigh Hunt (1784–1859) derived his theory of the imagination from Coleridge, his metaphorical method from Lamb and Hazlitt. Wellek indicates, however, that Hunt, in his introduction to *Imagination and Fancy* (1844), loses sight of Coleridge's idealistic epistemology and in *Wit and Humor* (1846) even equates comic wit with fancy. As a laudatory universalist, Hunt looked upon censoring criticism as an "impertinence," though he himself, a propagandist for "pure" poetry, expressed reservations about Dante's bigotry, Milton's gloom, Swift's coarseness, and Wordsworth's music. Unlike Saintsbury and Thorpe, Wellek sees Hunt as clearly inferior to Coleridge, Lamb, Hazlitt, De Quincey, and Carlyle. "He has little judgment, though a definite taste for the fairylike, the glowingly imaginative, or the sentimentally charming" (125).

As in his discussions of De Quincey and Hunt, Wellek tends to stress the limitations of the cocksure Whig historian Thomas Babington Macaulay (1800–59), only an occasional literary critic. A clear and vivid writer, he rarely showed interest in analysis or theory. Wellek's examination of the early essays—"Pope" (1824), "Milton" (1825), and "Dante" (1828)—reveals a scheme of the history of poetry which resembles Thomas Warton's double view of primitivism and progress, with poetry moving from the pictorial to the abstract, from Dante to Milton. Thus Macaulay, who dichotomizes image and sign, condemns the Neoclassical criticism that succeeded an age of imagination. His *History of England* (1848–61) treats Pope, Addison, and Goldsmith harshly. His essay "Samuel Johnson" (1831) proclaims that only a fool like Boswell could have written such a great biography. "These bundles of antitheses," says Wellek, "are both imperceptive as psychology and superficial as history" (130). While loyal to the Ancients, to Shakespeare, to Richardson, and to Jane Austen, Macaulay condemned Coleridge's "hocus-pocus" and Wordsworth's "twaddle." Macaulay's doctrinaire liberalism, like Jeffrey's, condemned such contemporaries as Carlyle, Melville, and Dickens. The grounds of Macaulay's literary judgment—no surprise—became increasingly obscure, arbitrary, "Philistine."

As with Macaulay, so with John Stuart Mill (1806–73). Literary criticism played second fiddle to other interests, but Wellek finds his early papers interesting. In "What Is Poetry?" (1833) Mill argues that poetry is soliloquy; feeling, not narrative; emotional truth, not naturalistic imitation; pure self-expression, not rhetoric. Wellek shows how in "The Two Kinds of Poetry" (1833) Mill expanded and modified this extreme position to include poets of nature (Shelley the spontaneous lyrical poet) and poets of culture (Wordsworth the deliberate unlyrical poet-philosopher). Thereafter, in his essays, reviews, and scattered pronouncements, Mill tried to reconcile poetry with knowledge. "There is genuine though perverse originality," Wellek contends, "in Mill's emphasis on soliloquy, which runs counter to the whole affective tradition of British aesthetics" (135).

Wellek displays representative literary opinions of John Ruskin (1819–1900), but decides, after all, that in a history of criticism the Victorian prophet's significance lies in his aesthetics of organism—in the first three volumes of *Modern Painters* (1843, 1846, 1856) and in the social importance he gives to art. For Ruskin, "poetry" included the work of poet, painter, and sculptor alike. Touching upon Ruskin's roots in German Romantic aesthetics (by way of Wordsworth, Coleridge, Carlyle, and others), Wellek outlines Ruskin's theory combining natural and supernatural, nature and symbol. Ruskin conceives of the penetrating, synthesizing, contemplating imagination as it realizes three artistic ideals: purist, grotesque, naturalist.

Wellek perceives that symbols to Ruskin became real. "However fantastic and superstitious this creed may strike us, it follows from the basic romantic animism which Ruskin, in different versions of literalness, embraced all his life" (145). According to Wellek, the capricious but famous attack on the "pathetic fallacy" denies the nature of metaphor or substitution, fosters literalness and "sincerity." Like many others, Ruskin came to confuse art with morality and religion, but he saw early the blight which industrialization inflicts on the great humanizing activity of art.

IV   *American Criticism: From Poe to Fuller*

Reacting against intellectual dependence on England, Americans during this time turned to the Continent, particularly to German Romanticists and historians and their British and French intermediaries. Wellek naturally sees the vantage point across the ocean as allowing American criticism to be "something like a synthesis of European criticism, exempt, at least, from the particular limitations of the main national traditions" (151). He devotes a chapter in *The Age of Transition* to Poe, Emerson, Thoreau, Margaret Fuller, and, curiously, Jones Very.

Unlike Baudelaire, Wellek does not characterize the frenetic Edgar Allan Poe (1809–1849) as an isolated genius. Rather, Wellek sees him as a successful literary journalist who reflected the taste of his time. Noting that many of Poe's 258 critical items are repetitious, biased, maudlin, or dull, Wellek makes a case for Poe's frequent rightness and occasional insight—as when he analyzes and champions Hawthorne and Dickens. Wellek naturally sees merit in Poe's claims for criticism, especially its judicial function. Poe appears in Wellek's *History* because of his highly influential "Philosophy of Composition" (1846) and "The Poetic Principle" (1850), along with *Marginalia* and scattered remarks in book reviews. By placing taste between intellect and the moral sense, Poe (like Kant) exalts the social role of art and of the beautiful.

Inventor of the term "the heresy of the Didactic," Poe readmitted truth and morality in the drama and the novel—for the sake of verisimilitude, says Wellek, not virtue. Poe's "beauty"—vague, suggestive, strange, sad—partakes also of Neoplatonic harmony, proportion, ideality, but in practice his view of "ideal" poetry is wider. Wellek interprets Poe's "music"—mellifluous sounds or mystic longing—as in no way symbolist, for Poe distrusts metaphor, simile, correspondence, analogy. Since imagination for the mystical-mathematical Poe is combinatory, not creative, he here followed neither A. W. Schlegel nor Coleridge: He "rejected the dialectical and symbolist creed and remained an 18th-century rationalist with occult leanings" (159). Wellek looks upon Poe's technological acrobatics in "The Philosophy of Composition" as a hoax, his remarks on effect as inadequate.

No "calculating" Poe, the "wisely passive" Ralph Waldo Emerson (1803–82) and his fellow Transcendentalists, as Wellek's earlier essays showed, expounded the concepts of Romantic symbol and creative imagination. Organic art in Emerson's monistic universe ciphers and embodies fluid natural divinity. From *Nature* (1836), the early and late *Essays*, and the *Journal*, Wellek quotes copious dicta ("Nature is a metaphor of the human mind") to exemplify Emerson's theory and method of the transforming imagination. In arguing for contemporaneity, democracy, and American art, Emerson pushes ultimately for religious equality, for all in each and each in all, for universal metamorphosis. A contradiction in Emerson's aesthetics, however, troubles Wellek. On the one hand, there is free, fluid symbolism; on the other, necessary classic beauty—a fixed relation between right words and right things, an unCarlylean disposition to worship facts, a trust in final goodness and harmony.

Emerson, to Wellek's dismay, also can exalt Homer and Shakespeare as inspired, impersonal seers and still confound them with general human vision, "sincerity," art in the mind of everybody. All poetry and all empathetic criticism fade into the One, and the immobile entity called literature has no history. Wellek notes that Emerson, a wide but unsystematic reader, had little use for Byron, Shelley, Jane Austen, Dickens, and Macaulay; he admired Milton, Burns, Herbert, Donne, Herrick, Marvell, Ben Jonson's songs, and Wordsworth's "Immortality Ode." He praised Shakespeare, but disparaged his role as master of revels. For Goethe (the source for his aesthetics) he had mixed reactions. In discussing Emerson's other Neoplatonic sources, Wellek once more concludes that the New Englander's combination, his angle of vision—unlike Coleridge's—is original: "Emerson is quintessential, and almost frightening in the purity of his doctrine" (176).

Of Emerson's three associates whose criticism Wellek treats briefly, Henry David Thoreau (1817–62) stands closest to the master.

Wellek displays quotations from Thoreau's journals that echo or intensify Emerson's notions. Thoreau's only long piece of literary criticism, "Thomas Carlyle and His Works" (1847), does not discriminate among the works; the critic praises Carlyle's sincerity but objects to his stylistic mannerisms. In the "Reading" chapter in *Walden* (1854), Thoreau extols the ancients, Western and Eastern. But, concludes Wellek, "Life absorbed his art: what place was there for criticism?" (178).

Though Jones Very (1813–80) claimed to write essays on Shakespeare by listening to the Holy Ghost, Wellek bemusedly hears "only the voices of Coleridge and August Wilhelm Schlegel muffled by pious declamations" (178). Wellek adds that Very on his way to truth and light "left literature, Shakespeare, and the text of *Hamlet* far behind" (179).

Margaret Fuller (1810–50) also abandoned criticism (for politics), but Wellek counts as a solid achievement her picturesque, often sentimental, work in the *Dial* (1840–44) and the *New York Daily Tribune* (1844–46). Her insight into American literary worth is more sure than her judgments on English and Continental work. She esteemed Poe and Hawthorne, for example, over Longfellow and Lowell. Wellek also appreciates her concrete reflections on criticism itself. Also original is Wellek's decision to associate her in spirit closer to Bettina von Arnim and George Sand than to Goethe and Emerson—"to the generous, frank, and somewhat overfervid spirit of Young Germany and liberal France" (181).

V   German Criticism: From Grillparzer to Marx and Engels

Wellek's miscellaneous chapter on German critics and historians tries to arrange them from most conservative to most innovative. Though devoid of speculative power, the classical Austrian dramatist Franz Grillparzer (1791–1872) defends his practice in his notebooks, denies a close connection between poetry and history, exalts genius, and deems the poet the best judge of poetry. The eight-volume collection of the eminent scholar-critic and poet Ludwig Uhland (1787–1862) contains unfinished projects on Middle High German literary history, a German mythology, and folklore studies, "but there is enough finished work to make Uhland, after the Grimms, the most distinguished early student of *Germanistik*" (188). In his books of literary history, the kindly Roman Catholic poet Joseph von Eichendorff (1788–1857) judges that *all* poetry has declined since the Middle Ages.

Wellek touches upon the ideological warfare surrounding the figure of Goethe in the work of Wilhelm von Humboldt (1767–1835), Carl Ernst Schubarth (1796–1861), and the Berlin cultists Varnhagen von Ense (1785–1858) and his wife, Rahel Levin (1771–1833). Of the early interpreters, Wellek judges the best to be Carl Gustav Carus (1789–1869), who struggled to view Goethe and his work as a totality. But in the crude yet eloquent *Die deutsche Literatur* (1828), the nationalistic Wolfgang Menzel (1798–1873) attacks Goethe for his retreat into Chinese studies, for his paganism and eclecticism. In *Tags- und Jahreshefte*, the radical journalist Ludwig Börne (1786–1837) attacks him for his political conservatism.

In *The Age of Transition,* Wellek contends that the evocative criticism, self-defining polemics, and exile prose of Heinrich Heine (1797–1856) survive today because of his popularity as a tough and witty poet whose late poems anticipate modern complexity. Heine praised the objective, the universal, the ironical—Aristophanes, Shakespeare, Cervantes, Molière, Sterne. He condemned much in German Romantic philosophy and French Romantic drama. Wellek sees in Heine's *Die romantishe Schule* (1833) a caustic counterpart to Madame de Staël's *De l'Allemagne*. He resolves the art-is-autonomous/art-is-life contradiction in Heine's curious theoretical position by appealing to his Hegelian-Schlegelian view of history: the autonomy of art is a postulate of a particular time. Though persecuted poet-prophets of a new age will merge art and life, Heine denounced the realist dogma: form, inborn symbolism, matters most—nature copying art. For Wellek, Heine's poetic theory is "transitional and ambivalent: romantic *and* liberal, aesthetic *and* didactic" (199).

Wellek tells of the bizarre suppression (1835–42) of four other literary men whom the German Diet specified as "Young Germany." In his derivative lectures, *Äesthetische Feldzüge* (1834), Ludolf Wienbarg (1802–72) pleaded for a "poetry of life," judged Goethe with a divided mind, and praised Heine's wit. Karl Gutzkow (1811–78), in books, pamphlets, and reviews which Wellek describes as "fuzzy, flabby, diffuse," called for big novels representing world variety and simultaneity; like others, Gutzkow admired Goethe's work while regretting his politics. Another publicist and debater, Heinrich Laub (1806–84), wrote superficial theatrical criticism (1829–75) and the shoddy *Geschichte der deutschen Literatur* (1839), more compilation than history. The least-known of the Young Ger-

mans today, Theodor Mundt (1808–61), seems to Wellek by far the
best critic and historian; unfortunately, Mundt's brilliant *Geschichte
der Literatur der Gegenwart* (1842) loses its original aim, becomes
too inclusive, too encyclopedic.

Though he finds Mundt's liberal position and historical method
similar to that of the eminent Georg Gottfried Gervinus (1805–71),
Wellek goes on to say that the dour historian of German literature
would be aghast to be grouped with Young Germany. Wellek's full
analysis of Gervinus's five-volume *Geschichte der poetischen Na-
tionalliteratur der Deutschen* (1835–42) reveals his repudiation of
aesthetic standards for explanations of the relation between poetry
and national evolution. Still, Gervinus's forgotten literary history,
combining history and criticism, seems to Wellek the best work
before Taine and De Sanctis. Only the unsympathetic chapter on
Romantic poetry is excessively polemical. In practice, German classicism informs Gervinus's aesthetic judgment; his sympathies lie
with Homer, Shakespeare, Lessing, and the Classical stage of
Goethe and Schiller. He prefers epic and tragedy over lyric and
didactic verse. Wellek stresses Gervinus's attitude toward the
unShakespearean Schiller, whose Germany lacked true history yet
reconciled Hellenism and Christianity. Gervinus's four-volume
Shakespeare (1849–50) surveys all the plays in detail. "Moral scrutiny becomes identical with a search for artistic unity" (212). In the
end, Wellek decides, Gervinus the moralist destroyed Gervinus the
critic.

Wellek's glance at the Hegelians tries to rescue what is still valuable. Carl Friedrich Göschel (1784–1862) and Herman Friedrich
Wilhelm Hinrichs (1794–1861) interpreted *Faust* simply as confir-
mation of Hegel's thought. Eduard Gans (1798–1839) interpreted
the end of *Hamlet* as the triumph of Reason. The early work of
Hermann Ulrici (1806–84) develops the idea of art, genre, and necessity. Heinrich Theodor Rötscher (1802–71), defending the Hegelian method, relentlessly dovetails all artistic details into his
leading idea. For Hegel's learned biographer, Karl Rosenkranz
(1805–79), German medieval literature passes triadically from intuition (epic) to sentiment (lyric) to thought (didactic poetry); Wellek
finds especially noteworthy Rosenkranz's pioneering volumes on
Diderot and his ingenious but unresolved *Aesthetik des Hässlichen*
(1853), where the ugly is to art what evil is to ethics and disease to
biology.

From Hegelianism the optimistic Friedrich Theodor Vischer

(1807–87) moved to psychologism, illustrating the new turn toward positivism. Wellek discusses Vischer's views on Goethe, Shakespeare, and his contemporaries; his monumental six-volume compendium *Äesthetik oder Wissenschaft des Schönen* (1846–57); and his last paper, "Das Symbol" (1887). Unlike Hegel, Vischer in his *Äesthetik* devotes attention to natural beauty; sees art not implicated in historical necessity; emphasizes image over idea; elevates the comic to the highest genre; substitutes a conflict between the plastic and the pictorial for Hegel's Symbolic, Classical, and Romantic styles; and sees not the end but the decline of art. Of the later revisions, Wellek declares: "Symbolism is the basis of all art: but in Vischer it means primarily empathy, animation of nature, anthropomorphism, and thus supports a pantheistic metaphysics" (222). Following up a hint from Croce, Wellek also observes the anti-Hegelian reaction in the work of Theodor Wilhelm Danzel (1818–50), a man of good sense, who abhors the confusion of art and religion, intellectualism, and the assumption that the poet's worldview is systematic. Though Danzel desired criticism on the individuality of artworks, comparison of sources, and literary history based on poetic conceptions, in the end he settled down to pure "research."

Turning to the once-eminent Friedrich Hebbel (1813–63), Wellek examines "Mein Work über das Drama" (1843) and Hebbel's preface to his tragedy *Maria Magdalena* (1844). To the old view of man's defeat by the universe, Hebbel gives an original twist: "the individual is not punished for his revolt or *hubris* or lack of measure, but . . . perishes simply because he is an individual" (226). Though Hebbel frowned on contemporary patriotic historical drama, he reflected on tragedy's relation to history and to the present: on universal conflicts between the sexes, the state and the individual, man and society. In the proud and stoic Hebbel, Wellek sees neither Hegel's optimism nor Schopenhauer's pessimism. Rather, he discerns a trace of Kant's higher law lifting the individual above his doom.

Quoting mostly from the first and second volumes of the *Collected Works* (1846), Wellek sees Arnold Ruge (1802–1880) as the most vocal of the Hegelian left, a critic who combined historicism with radicalism and relativism with progress. Literature for Ruge reflects *and* aids the process toward freedom. The poet reflects *and* changes his age. Wellek indicates that though Ruge admired Goethe and Schiller, he deplored their stress on self-realization and individual culture. Romanticism to Ruge was the enemy of reason; reason alone unites the ideal (poetry) with the real (politics). Wellek nicely translates Ruge's witty twelve-point Romantic credo.

Ruge was a signal source for the scattered literary pronouncements of Karl Marx (1818–83) and Friedrich Engels (1820–95). Their enunciations, Wellek jibes, "have been treated by Marxist critics in the same way that canonical texts are interpreted and elaborated by theologians" (233). Wellek touches on Marx's early years as a student of the classics and of Neoclassical German aesthetics. Wellek exhibits contradictions in *Die deutsche Ideologie* (1845–46) and argues that history does not support Marx's claim that the full-time master artist will disappear in the new classless society. Wellek traces Marx's view in the *Communist Manifesto* (1847–48) that intellectual life changes *with* economic change to his view in *Kritik der politischen Ökonomie* (1859) that intellectual life changes *because* of economic change. In the Marx-Engels epistolary debate with Ferdinand Lassalle (1825–64), Wellek sees nothing exceptional. Only Engels's letters after Marx's death lend oracular support to today's full-blown Marxist theory, which "still shows traces of the strange medley of radical ideology, Hegelian dialectics, economic determinism, and realist typology found in the occasional pronouncements of its spiritual fathers" (239).

VI   Russian Criticism: From Pushkin to Belinsky

Wellek views Russian criticism, in part, as a laboratory for the radical solution of literary problems. Glancing at early echoes of French and later of English and German ideas, he touches upon several contributors, but gives the lion's share of his brief Introductory to the great, independent poet Alexander Pushkin (1799–1837). Siding with Romanticism while preserving a feeling for symmetry and harmony, Pushkin "could hardly conceive of the poet as an idle singer of an idle day," Wellek asserts, "but neither could he think of him as a mouthpiece of authority or the servant of the immediate communal need" (243).

The Age of Transition closes with the highly important and effective, the temperamental and authoritative, Vissarion Belinsky (1811–48). To his great credit, Belinsky defined the achievement of such writers of his time as Pushkin, Gogol, Lermontov, Dostoevsky, Turgenev, Goncharov, and Nekrasov. On the debit side, he underestimated Russian folklore and eighteenth-century literature, discredited some fine poets around Pushkin, and overpraised Scott, Cooper, Béranger, and George Sand. Wellek stresses the historical importance of Belinsky's theory—deriving as it does from the Germans. Like others, Belinsky modified Romantic conceptions, adapting German idealism to Russian reality.

Wellek sympathetically traces Belinsky's shifting accents in his celebrated articles, from the series *Literary Reveries* (1834) to "A Look at Russian Literature in 1847" (1848). Belinsky at times stressed art as organic wholeness, at times as historical product. Wellek recites the paradoxes of the middle period—when Belinsky saw (and wrongly foresaw) no conflict between aesthetic and historical criticism. His politically radical late work recants arguments in his early work and blames earlier Russian literary failures on a more vicious age—a belief in inevitable progress which Wellek finely labels Belinsky's "mystique of time" (248). In battling a hostile political regime, Belinsky necessarily adulterated his literary criticism, advocating (in his own brand of journalese) popular techniques of social realism. Still, to Wellek's mind, Belinsky preserved his basic sensibility and critical insight, deteriorating as a literary critic, however, the more he fixed on extraliterary "time," "progress," "reality," and "society."

VII   *French Criticism: From Balzac to Hennequin*

The Later Nineteenth Century, Wellek's big fourth volume, reveals how such great critics as De Sanctis, Nietzsche, and James made a bridge to the twentieth century. Wellek begins with a discussion of French Realist, Naturalist, and Impressionist critics. He devotes a chapter to Taine and then takes up literary historians and minor French critics. Next, Wellek focuses on De Sanctis and surveys Italian criticism after him. The English historians and theorists follow. After his discussion of the Americans, Wellek discusses the Russian radical and conservative critics. He illuminates German criticism, particularly the ideas of Dilthey. A chapter on Georg Brandes the Dane precedes chapters on the English critics Swinburne, Symonds, Wilde, Saintsbury, and Shaw. This volume ends with the French Symbolists, Baudelaire and Mallarmé.

To begin, Wellek elucidates the term "realism." His discussion of the preface to the *Comédie humaine* (1842) and the early article "Des Artistes" (1830) touches upon a few of the various and ranging literary opinions of Honoré de Balzac (1799–1850). Conscious indeed of the whirligig of fashion, Balzac in his *La Muse du departement* (1843) calls for a criticism based on textual understanding, on principles, on system. But where the Marxist critic Lukács finds Balzac profound, Wellek finds him only interesting, as in his triadic classification (imagery, ideas, eclecticism) of contemporary writers and their literature and of his self-classification in the misnamed third group. Because the great social novelist lacks "detachment," Balzac is for Wellek neither a realist nor even a forerunner of realism.

Unlike Balzac, the stylist Gustave Flaubert (1821–81) strove, as all students of literature know, for "impersonality," a technical device which passed over into *impassibilité*, detachment, indifference. Thus in his search for *le mot juste*, Flaubert wavered between scientism and aestheticism. Examining Flaubert's impressive aesthetics in *Lettres à George Sand* (1884) and *Correspondence* (1887), Wellek defends the illusionist Flaubert against "engaged" writers like Sartre. Though the power of Zola's Naturalism often impressed Flaubert, more often its materialism and narrowness offended him. Flaubert's "impersonality" Wellek likens to Keats's "chameleon poet" and Diderot's internalizing actor. Flaubert envisioned the critic as artist, the individual work as the center of stylistic attention, and literary history as strictly *literary*. When Flaubert grasps the unity of form and content, subject and object, he comes nearest to reconciling his own involvement and detachment, his Romanticism and Realism—as Wellek discerns in the famous scene of the agricultural show in *Madame Bovary*.[7] This synthesis Flaubert's disciple Guy de Maupassant (1850–93) managed, but on a lower level. Wellek notes, however, that Maupassant's several prefatorial insistences on objectivity are at odds with his illusionist and solipsistic assumptions.

In the late 1860s—well before *Le Roman expérimental* (1880)— Émile Zola had formulated Naturalism as a form of scientific determinism. Unlike literalists who upbraid Zola for his false identification of novelist and physician, Wellek makes clear the equation: he sees it as a ruse to gain prestige for imaginative literature, to free the novelist, allowing him to treat any subject without charges of immorality. More exasperating to Wellek are Zola's Philistine attacks on great writers before Balzac and Stendhal. While praising Daudet, Maupassant, and the early Huysmans—as well as the early Impressionist painters—Zola condemned the polite timidities of poetry and the theater, of Sainte-Beuve and Taine. But Wellek also shows that Zola admired Turgenev and Tolstoy—as did the conservative French nobleman Melchior de Vogüé (1848–1910), who in *Le Roman russe*

(1886) presented Turgenev and Tolstoy as Christian antidotes to Zola's immorality and scientific indifference.

Wellek finds it difficult to distinguish between the basic theories of Jules Lemaître (1853–1914) and Anatole France (1844–1924). "Both come from Renan's scepticism and dilettantism and continue the sceptical side of Sainte-Beuve" (22).[8] Wellek deems Lemaître the better critic, France the better writer. The subjectivist Lemaître applied the modernist painter's term "impressionism" to criticism (personal enjoyment) and only in the end recognized that criticism is judgment. In the *Préface* to the first volume of *La Vie littéraire* (1888), the witty and graceful Anatole France made his famous argument for complete subjectivism, for the critic as one who "tells the adventures of his soul among masterpieces." Like Lemaître, he defined taste but deplored Naturalism and dogma. "What was important, besides the radical anti-theory, both in Lemaître and France, was rather the form: the perfection they attained in critical *causerie*" (26).

Objections to the race-milieu-moment doctrine of Hippolyte Taine (1828–93) are to Wellek tenable but simple. Though Taine lacked order and evidence, Wellek does not naively dismiss the elusive concepts of "race" and "moment." Most useful today is "milieu," actually the old practice of explaining literature by its environment. In "climate," Wellek sees a less strict causal explanation than in "audience." Though Bernard Weinberg asserted that Wellek, typically, analyzed no single text in this chapter,[9] the fact is that he quite systematically and inventively analyzes Taine's four-volume *Histoire de la littérature anglaise* (1864). The "scientific" Taine, however, seems to Wellek more pantheistic than materialistic or positivistic: Wellek insists that in terms of epistemology, history, and aesthetics, Taine is basically Hegelian. Unlike Hegel, however, Taine is a pessimist, believing in scientific but not in moral or artistic progress. To him art is sensuous knowledge, a "representation" of its age and nation, a summary of history. In Taine's criticism, says Wellek, German historicity and French psychology meet.

Wellek notes that Taine's scale of lowest-to-highest (fashion, generation, period, race, humanity) seems to contradict his notion of the concrete universal as the highest art. Often Taine draws evidence indiscriminately—from fiction, history, and documents. In literature he admires strong social heroes, ranking them from local to universal, from realistic to ideal—thus not really reconciling ethics and aesthetics. In Taine's scheme the soul or mind of the writer seems to Wellek overly dominated by a "master faculty." Rarely interested in biography, Taine often misidentifies a writer with his characters. Sincerity often becomes his standard for genuine poetry, blinding him to craft and unity.

From his early *La Fontaine* (1853) to his late *L'Ancien Régime* (1875), Taine lauded the "characteristic" English, condemned the "classic" French. He praised the poets of the Romantic Age (especially Musset), the novels of Stendhal and Balzac, and he tended, says Wellek, to overpraise the North, except when influenced by French Neoclassicism. Because Taine saw man as basically irrational, he minimized the intellectual life. Preoccupied with nationality, he reveals to Wellek little sense of the totality of European literary tradition or comparative literature. Nor did the science-minded Taine treat the work of art as an object in a comparative series. In tracing to Taine's pessimism his preference for the sentimental, Wellek sees Taine himself as a representative figure—a complex mind at the crossroads of the century.

Wellek delineates the eclipsed reputation of Ferdinand Brunetière (1849–1906), powerful editor of *Revue des Deux Mondes*. Surprisingly, this defender of French Classicism applied Darwinian evolutionary principles to genre study. Wellek, as usual, detects some injustice done Brunetière. *Le Roman naturaliste* (1883), for example, does more than assail Zola and Naturalism. Wellek first points out Brunetière's sympathetic, if imaginatively awkward, analyses of works by Flaubert, Daudet, Maupassant, and George Eliot, and then he details the critic's insights into *Madame Bovary*. Wellek indicates that Brunetière liked what he deemed the right kind of realism and that he understood symbolism rightly. But his distaste for Baudelaire the man, for example, caused him to judge the poet unfairly.

Wellek sees Brunetière's strength in theoretical criticism, especially in the history of literature. "No critic, at least in France, has stated so clearly what seems to be central, critical truths" (61). Criticism must distinguish literary study from other disciplines, must focus on the work itself, must explicate, classify, compare, judge, and rank. Wellek, as opposed as Brunetière to scientism and impressionism, still doubts Brunetière's absolute divorce between sympathy and judgment. Brunetière's Neoclassical purity of genre derives, according to Wellek, from his keen sense of history and evolution. But the institution of genre does not die biologically, as do individuals and even species (ontology). Most successful of Bru-

netière's evolutionary schemes, often discussed by Wellek elsewhere, is his rather rigid arrangement of generic representations—
as biologists arrange phylogenetically the "brain" from fish to man.
Sceptical of such biological analogies as the struggle for existence
among genres and transformation of one genre into another, Wellek
yet discerns that Brunetière has wrestled with a crucial problem in
the history of literature as a changing art.

The historian next takes up the work of the great positivist Gustave
Lanson (1857–1934) and a few bold synthesizers. Lanson symbolizes
for Wellek academic literary history in France. Wellek approves of
Lanson's prestigious often-revised *Histoire de la littérature française*
(1894). Its direct criticism of texts and writers makes it more than
a first-rate manual, but its anti-symbolism harms Lanson's reputation
today. Important in the expansion of nineteenth-century French
literary historiography are the medievalist Gaston Paris (1839–1903),
the prolific Émile Faguet (1847–1916), the cultured historian
Jacques Jusserand (1855–1932), the aesthetic-minded Auguste An-
gellier (1847–1911), and the graceful stylist of English literary history
Émile Legouis (1861–1937). Finally, Wellek offers as "a major postulate of a new age" the grand view of Joseph Texte (1865–1900) that
littérature comparée should study all literatures.[10]

Of the well-known minor French critics of the time, Wellek sin-
gles out in his wide-ranging fourth chapter a few diverse individuals.
In the violent, flamboyant seventeen-volume *Les Oeuvres et les
hommes* (1860–1909) of conservative Jules Barbey d'Aurevilly
(1808–89), Wellek senses "the support of a fervently held positive
creed and of a taste that allows him enthusiasms and recognitions
which are sometimes perceptive and even prophetic" (81). Among
other things, Wellek contrasts d'Aurevilly's admiration for Baudelaire with the loathing of Edmond Scherer (1815–89), the erstwhile
Protestant theologian who selected from his *Le Temps* articles his
ten-volume *Études critique sur la littérature contemporaine* (1863–95).

Like d'Aurevilly and Scherer, the versatile Émile Montegut
(1826–95) contrasted godless French Naturalism with Christian English Realism. An intermediary among Western literatures, he is seen
best in *Types littéraires* (1882). He wrote skillful, often paradoxical
essays for *Revue des Deux Mondes*, but "he lacks the strong individuality, either as a theorist or a judge, which alone conveys a
name to posterity" (86). Wellek finds the diagnostic confessions of
Taine's heir, critic-novelist Paul Bourget (1852–1935), impressive
though overdrawn and mechanical. The historian depicts the two-

volume *Essais de psychologie contemporaine* (1883, 1885), in which
Bourget traces the source of modern decadence. New is Wellek's
attempt to rehabilitate the almost-forgotten Émile Hennequin
(1859–88) as a precursor of the current interest in audience; in a
rare personal note, Wellek explains that F. X. Šalda "translated him
and kept his memory green in my student years at the University
of Prague in the 1920's"(92).[11]

VIII Italian Criticism: From De Sanctis to Verga

The History of Italian Literature (1870–71) by Francesco De Sanctis (1817–83) is for Wellek "the finest history of any literature ever
written" (124). His chapter on De Sanctis, highly praised in Italy,
offers plausible reasons for the neglect of *the* Italian critic outside
Italy. Amply quoting the complex and patriotic De Sanctis, Wellek
makes plain those doctrines on autonomy and form so fervently
defended by Croce and others. "This aesthetic of an organic, concrete, individual work of art, in which form and content are ideally
indistinguishable, created by genius in an act of imagination, is
matched," observes Wellek, "by an analogous theory of criticism"
(100). The critical act demands first submission, then recreation,
finally judgment.

Indeed, Wellek's De Sanctis is neither monist nor materialist,
neither incipient Marxist nor Crocean. Wellek elucidates De Sanctis's variations on the interpenetration of artistic elements. De Sanctis, as Wellek shows, praises Manzoni and Zola, condemns ruinous
irony and comedy, and prefers the objective art of Homer or Ariosto
to the subjective art of Petrarch or Tasso. De Sanctis elevates drama
to the highest form, cares little for minor genres, and views ideal
style as determined by the "thing" that wants expression. Rejecting
art for art's sake, De Sanctis favors the whole "poet" to the partial
"artist."

De Sanctis's great two-volume literary *History*, his many *Saggi
critici* (1874), and his lectures at Naples (1871–76) constitute a history
of Italy's fall and redemption. In De Sanctis's story of the complex
march of mind from medieval transcendence to secular immanen-
tism, Wellek notes some contradictions, distortions, and omissions.
But mainly Wellek delights in De Sanctis's integration of close criticism and broad history. In this scheme Wellek finds no linear
literary progress, only dissolution and reunification: "Content and
form, fused in Dante at his best, dissolves to be fused again in

Manzoni and Leopardi" (116). Resorting to German terms, Wellek
outlines De Sanctis's trust in *Weltgeist, Zeitgeist,* and *Volksgeist,*
an arrangement which enables Wellek to summarize the impact of
German thought, particularly dualism and Kantianism, on De Sanctis. Like Belinsky in Russia and Taine in France, De Sanctis in Italy
adapted to his time and place his distinct fusion of Hegelian historicism and Romantic aesthetics. At the De Sanctis Congress in
Naples in 1977, Wellek read in Italian his paper "De Sanctis e il
Realismo" (1978).

Wellek's miscellaneous chapter on other Italian critics shows that
in spite of De Sanctis's brilliant fusion of history and criticism, an
erudite "historical school" appeared in Italy. Wellek's refrain is not
unfamiliar: "There is much learning acquired with enormous diligence, much organizational power, much acumen . . . but also a
strange incapacity for aesthetic analysis or even sensitive reaction,
a lack of insight into critical problems, which they share, of course,
with the whole trend of positivistic scholarship of the time, whether
in Germany or France or the United States" (127–28). The diffuse
Francesco Torraca (1853–1938) and the bizarre Vittorio Imbriani
(1840–86), however, clung to some of De Sanctis's central doctrine.

But dominating the Italian literary scene was the poet, public
figure, and critic Giosuè Carducci (1835–1907). In *Storia del Giorno*
(1892), for instance, he "goes constantly beyond the assumptions of
the historical school in the direction of both a speculative literary
history and a judicial analytical criticism" (132). Wellek points out
the conflict in Carducci between aesthetic and ideological predilec-
tions and then discusses some figures around him. In a general
history of criticism neither the limited theory of Italian Naturalism
voiced by the literary journalist-novelist Luigi Capuana (1839–1915)
nor the few sober pronouncements of its best fiction writer, Giovanni
Verga (1840–1922), seem considerable, yet Wellek manages to epitomize the appeal and the tone of these champions of *verismo.*

IX   *English Criticism: From Dallas to Stephen*

English criticism for Wellek reached a low point around 1850.
Victorian didacticism and moralism, however, found opponents in
new historicism, classicism, realism, and aesthetics. "But these
motives are not clearly set off from one another: they combine, they
enter into compromises, they attempt genuine syntheses" (141).
Wellek illuminates the chief virtues and defects of key works by
several English scholars, compared to whom the triadic-minded

Eneas Sweetland Dallas (1828–79) stands almost alone.

In his patchy *Poetics* (1852) and unfinished two-volume *The Gay Science* (1866), the now-neglected Dallas erected what Wellek humorously refers to as a Victorian Crazy Castle. "The incongruous mixture of psychology of the unconscious with insistently symmetrical schematization makes Dallas's books piquant dishes not to be missed by connoisseurs of the history of criticism" (145). Similarly, Wellek indicates that in *Principles of Success in Literature* (1865) George Henry Lewes (1817–78)—popular "classical" philosopher and first English champion of Realism—tried to make criticism scientific, a view to which Lewes specialist Alice R. Kaminsky takes exception.[12]

Like Lewes, the emotional but anti-sentimental novelist George Eliot advocated realism in her effective prefaces and essays. Appealing to Wellek's New Critical sympathies is George Eliot's fragment "Form in Art" (1868), in which she abortively speculates on the criterion of "complexity." In reference to the often-praised George Meredith essay "On the Idea of Comedy and the Uses of the Comic Spirit" (1877), Wellek agrees with Croce that in literary criticism psychological classifications "lead nowhere . . ." (153). Finally, in Robert Browning's rhapsodic essay on Shelley and in Gerard Manley Hopkins's sundry reflections, perfunctorily treated, Wellek discerns self-defenses of important poetic practices—in Browning universalizing individuality, in Hopkins metrical counterpoint.

The position of Matthew Arnold (1822–88) as the most important English critic of the second half of the nineteenth century seems to Wellek secure. "Arnold's advocacy of the critical spirit, of an atmosphere conducive to the free exchange of ideas, his praise of objectivity, disinterestedness, and curiosity (properly understood) are valuable and sound even today" (157). Primarily an historical critic, Arnold in *On the Study of Celtic Literature* (1867) and in other works addresses himself, like Taine, to questions of race and moment ("stream of history"). Wellek substantially details Arnold's conception of poetry as diluted religion, as didactic criticism of life, as a kind of Wordsworthian knowledge. Poetic interpretation of the natural and the moral world must be concrete for Arnold, but his "imaginative reason" differs from Neoclassical poetic reason. That Arnoldian "high seriousness" means *joy* rather than *solemnity* is Wellek's intriguing notion.

To be sure, Wellek exposes Arnold's contradictions, particularly his laxity regarding form and content, totality and detail, art and life. Too often Arnold conceives of subject and style as something fixed outside, a hard artistic vessel of form, as when Arnold fails to perceive the unifying principle in Tolstoy's *Anna Karenina*. Wellek hauls over the coals Arnold's eleven pedantic "touch-stones"—atomistic applications to other poetry of isolated passages from Homer, Milton, and Shakespeare. But, typically, Wellek does not indict "The Study of Poetry" (1888) wholesale. Rather, he ranks Arnold's essays and points out virtues and faults, particularly on Arnold's view of German literature. Adroitly, Wellek contrasts the Sainte-Beuvean *Essays in Criticism:* (1867) with more authoritative and judicial *Essays in Criticism: Second Series* (1888). Finally, he directs our attention to Arnold's once-influential ranking of Wordsworth, Byron, Keats, Shelley, and Coleridge. Wellek agrees with Arnold's defense of Wordsworth as the greatest, but not of Arnold's ranking Byron second. Today Keats, Shelley, and Coleridge seem far greater than Byron.

The limited Tory critic Walter Bagehot (1826–77) and the eminent Victorian Leslie Stephen (1832–1904) appear in Wellek's *History* as an appendix to Arnold. By drawing on Romantic notions of nature and imagination, Bagehot occasionally transcended his ideal of "normal" art. Compared to Shakespeare and Scott, most writers seemed eccentric to Bagehot, no real Neohumanist in Wellek's view. But Bagehot the practical critic, says G. N. G. Orsini, deserves more credit than Wellek gives him.[13] Still, Wellek, chiefly interested in what critics contribute to Western criticism, remarks judiciously on Bagehot's dubious classification of pure, ornate, and grotesque art; on his original twist to the concept of "type"; and on his interesting proposal for the word *literatesque* (on the analogy of picturesque). Wellek sees as inflated the early reputation of Virginia Woolf's father, Leslie Stephen. Wellek points out Stephen's superficial resemblances to Arnold. Simply put, Stephen values poets and novelists according to their tacit doctrines of bleak morality. Sometimes skillful, the criticism of this distinguished intellectual historian lacks clear aesthetic standards, a theory of literature, analytical techniques. Stephen's basic mistrust of art and criticism accounts, surmises Wellek, for the current disregard of his criticism.

X *American Criticism: From Whitman to James*

Because the manifestoes of Walt Whitman (1819–92) about individual intuition really stem from Quakerism, the Enlightenment, and Transcendentalism, Wellek finds the poet's total rejection of the European past deceptive. Carefully the historian outlines not only the Emerson-Whitman relationship, but Whitman's supposed admiration for Hegel and his pains to identify *Leaves of Grass* (1855) with prestigious German idealism. Whitman has a concept and a program for poetry as well as an ideal of the poet, but Wellek, playing down the German Connection, sees in Whitman's "monstrous syncretism" (192) not coherent metaphysics, aesthetics, or theory. "Like many others, he preaches contemporaneity, naturalism, and realism; but with him these slogans are in the service not of a critical, social realism (as it was formulated in France and Russia) but of a poetry of the future, a worship of nature, of the world, America, the masses, science, and technology" (194).

In his original assessment of the Prefaces and Postscripts to *Leaves of Grass, Democratic Vistas* (1871), and other prose, Wellek traces Whitman's rhythmical and exclamatory prose-poetry to his spread-eagle equality and freedom, to his desire in literature for the archetypal American. Wellek cites Whitman's "democratic" objections to English literature, even to his favorite English writers—Shakespeare, Scott, Tennyson, and Carlyle. Still, in Whitman's post–Civil War call for literary continuity (for diverse poetries as one poetry), Wellek senses nostalgia for the European past.

As the first American scholar-critic, the learned, humane, and cosmopolitan James Russell Lowell (1819–91) naturally would appeal to a scholar-critic like René Wellek. Add Lowell's study of Coleridge, Lamb, Hazlitt, Goethe, and A. W. Schlegel—add Lowell's derivative theory of creative imagination, unity of form and content, objective aesthetic standard modified by historical considerations, universality of meaning—and the appeal is increased. But in spite of all Lowell's "erudition, brilliance, wit, and good taste," Wellek acknowledges, "his critical work has faded inexorably" (200). Wellek details how in practice Lowell's essays on Thoreau, Lessing, Dryden, Chaucer, Pope, Rousseau, and Wordsworth fail for want of coherence, skillful analysis, powerful characterization, and a steady point of view. The author of *Among My Books* (1870) and *My Study Windows* (1871) is for Wellek no true Neohumanist and, despite his picturesque similes, no impressionistic critic.

For the America of his day, the influential William Dean Howells (1837–1920), editor of *Atlantic Monthly* and *Harper's Magazine*, formulated a theory of realism, wrote many novels himself, and championed such writers as Henry James, Hamlin Garland, and

Stephen Crane. As a critical middleman, Howells preferred Russian, Italian, Spanish, and English realism over French naturalism. Though Howells's first book of criticism, *Modern Italian Poets* (1887), is "colorless," Wellek comments that the author "had the good taste to quote De Sanctis at crucial points . . ." (207). Drawing chiefly on *Criticism and Fiction* (1891), *My Literary Passions* (1895), and *Heroines of Fiction* (1901), Wellek describes Howells's central concerns: the objective point of view, fidelity to contemporary American life, the concrete universal, didactic illusionism. For Howells the novel and the romance are superior to the "romantistic" novel—Tolstoy and Hawthorne superior to Dickens and Hugo. Wellek appreciates Howells's theoretical inclusiveness, though he judges the critical performance generally lax. "Grossly exaggerated praise for trivial women short-story writers alternates with severe censure of the greatest masters" (211–12).

Rejecting both T. S. Eliot's disparagement and R. P. Blackmur's exaltation of the literary criticism of the master artist Henry James (1843–1916), Wellek sees him as the best American critic of the nineteenth century, bridging for the English-speaking world organistic aesthetics to modern criticism—a pronouncement which one reviewer looks forward to seeing vindicated in the final volumes.[14] As criticism, James's celebrated Prefaces to the New York Edition of his work disappoint Wellek. Less "cavalier"[15] is his view of the totality of James's achievement—from his *Nation* reviews (1864) to his articles on the "New Novel" (1914)—as remarkably coherent. By combining Anglo-American morality and French aesthetics, James for a time had hoped to become, Wellek amply shows, the American Sainte-Beuve.

This splendid exegesis depicts James chiding the English and European aesthetes for moral obtuseness. Nor is James a simple "Realist," though he calls for specificity and praises Balzac, Flaubert, Maupassant, Daudet, Turgenev, and George Eliot. Art is a selection *from* life, not a slice *of* life. James admired much unrealistic art and the "authority" of the literary illusionist. In James's view the "actual" of other lives helps civilize us, gives us experience and self-knowledge. Though James pleaded for freedom—not license—in art, he retreated, in Wellek's opinion, from *both* perverse and healthy physicality.

Distinguishing sharply between genres, James conceived of the lyric as intense personal expression: thus Wellek can accept James's criticism of Lowell as too literary, but not his criticism of Whitman as too barbaric. In sharp detail, Wellek discusses James's insistence on objectivity and illusion, his condemnation of first-person narrative and factual autobiography, his elimination of the omniscient narrator by applying techniques of the well-made drama to fiction, and his unifying "picture" and "idea" by the proper alternation of narrative, description, and dialogue. In turn, Wellek takes up James's concept of "foreshortening," the quality of the observer or "reflector," and type as the universal concrete.

In connection with this last concept, Wellek suggests that James underrates Emma Bovary as the type of the disillusioned romantic. Though James focuses on character psychology, he preaches—Wellek argues—the inseparability of character and action, form and content. Still, Wellek must defend the structure of *War and Peace,* for James tends to separate "form and life-content when confronted with works of art in a different tradition" (233). Also, Wellek rightly judges that James's insistence on a single point of view is too rigid. The adept windup fixes on James's shifting use of "style" and "texture," his advocacy of tonal unity, and, finally, his aesthetic and temperamental similarity to Goethe.

XI *Russian Criticism: From Chernyshevsky to Tolstoy*

Wellek devotes a brace of fine chapters—suggestive if not definitive—to the Russian radicals and conservatives. Unlike Belinsky, the radicals had no respect for German Romantic aesthetics. Paradoxically, says Wellek, they combined deterministic materialism with social reform. Nikolay Chernyshevsky (1828–89) lacks not only mature aesthetic sensibility, but also belief in the social role of art. Wellek quotes extensively from Chernyshevsky's crude *Aesthetic Relations of Art to Reality* (1855) and ends: "Here, surely, aesthetics has reached its nadir: or rather it has been asked to commit suicide" (240). Though obviously rejecting Chernyshevsky's complete identity of art and life, Wellek accepts the Russian's view of the unity of theory and history, his claims for Belinsky as literary historian, and some of his insights into Pushkin, Gogol, and Tolstoy.

Art for Chernyshevsky's disciple Nikolay Dobrolyubov (1836–61) also held little interest, though he was a more important theorist than his master. Still, Wellek sees him as "even more lumpish and stodgy . . . strangely unctuous in his violently secular way" (245).

Wellek quotes copiously, neatly stating his principle of selection:
"Thus Dobrolyubov runs the gamut from complete pessimism to
messianic hopes: from the view that literature is a passive mirror
to the view that it incites to direct action, transforms society" (247).
Wellek outlines Dobrolyubov's criteria as a "national" point of view,
"naturalness" over unity and coherence, and an emphasis on "content." Failing to retain his insights into "social types," the didactic
Russian nevertheless has advanced the earlier French and German
discussions of social types as revealing their author's unconscious
world-view—whatever the professed intention. But to expose Dobrolyubov's insensitive polemical method of abstraction, Wellek qui-
etly dissects the well-known "What is Oblomovism?" (1859) and
"The Realm of Darkness" (1860), the more subtle "When will the
day come?" (1860), and the last article, "Forgotten People" (1861),
published in the year of Dobrolyubov's death at age twenty-five.

Although Soviet historians tend to view Dobrolyubov's rival Dmi-
tri Pisarev (1840–68) as a radical individualist, Wellek sees him as
a rationalist working toward the common good via a scientific in-
telligentsia. Pisarev sees as outmoded the idea of organic development, the role of the imagination, aesthetic wholeness, the
distinction between life and fiction, inspiration, and unconscious
creation. Only novels and dramas—propaganda for realists ("thinking workers")—might be of limited use for "economic regeneration"
(socialism). Wellek groups Pisarev "with that long line of thinkers
that begins with Plato, goes through the Elizabethan puritans, the
'geometrical' partisans of the Moderns under Louis XIV, to the
Benthamite Utilitarians and men like Proudhon, who wanted to
banish the poets from the Republic" (256). Wellek detects in Pisarev,
the best of the radical critics, genuine insights, analytical power,
and a lively wit, support for which one finds more in Wellek's subtle
discussions of Pisarev's readings of Heine and Turgenev rather than
of Pushkin, Dostoevsky, and Tolstoy. While stressing the narrow
embattled utilitarianism of these radical critics, Wellek acknowledges their importance in the formation of the modern social novel.

Preoccupied with social types also, Apollon Grigoriev (1822–64)
excels the radicals in theoretical awareness and literary perception.
Wellek explicates for the first time in the West this Russian's Schellingian "organic" criticism. Unlike the radical critics esteemed in
the Soviet Union, Grigoriev rejects the belief in abstract humanity,
progress and reason, and historical relativism as a substitute for
aesthetic laws, for true historical sense. But Wellek remarks on the

unresolved conflict in Grigoriev's thought "between the Platonic and static absolute of emanationism and the evolutionism which he embraces in practice and which underlies his whole history of Russian 19th-century literature" (268–69). Briefly, Wellek illuminates Grigoriev's toleration of fallacious contemporary Realism, as well as his views on Belinsky, Pushkin, Gogol, and others.

Over Grigoriev today towers his one great disciple: Fyodor Dostoevsky (1821–81). Though the novelist's little-known literary criticism strikes Wellek as "sweetly reasonable," Dostoevsky's aesthetics strikes him as "extravagantly idealistic." So strained is his celebration of beauty "that we feel the kinship between the aesthetic ecstasy and the mystical illumination sometimes associated with the epileptic fit" (271). For Wellek this attitude clearly explains Dostoevsky's rejection of Realism, his quest for the eternal, the type, his praise for E. T. A. Hoffmann and Pushkin, his polemics against the Utilitarians.

The versatile Nikolay Strakhov (1828–96), though limited by his Grigorievan scheme, is for Wellek a sane and lucid critic of Russian literature of the 1860s and 1870s, particularly of Turgenev and Tolstoy. Besides handling Russian ideological criticism, Wellek touches on consequential academic scholarship little known in the West, especially Alexander Potebnya's (1836–91) identification of linguistics with poetry (anticipating symbolist and formalist poetry) and Alexander Veselovsky's (1838–1906) heroic but aesthetically deficient methodology of studying literature as a totality of works ("historical poetics").

To reveal the resolute affective and emotionalist criticism of Leo Tolstoy (1828–1910), Wellek describes and analyzes the famous *What Is Art?* (1898). Acknowledging its absurdities, he sees it, however, as no Christian conversional "aberration." Rather, this short late book exalting sincerity, infectious good emotions, and honest reproduction of reality is a logical—albeit radical—result of Tolstoy's basic primitivism: his antipathy to professional artists, obscurantist invention, and objective tradition. As in his chapter on Wordsworth, Wellek notes Tolstoy's Rousseauistic humanitarianism. Attacking modern art, Tolstoy "simply denies that art which is not universally comprehensible is art at all" (284). Since art is immediately knowable, criticism is superfluous. His own criticism, for example, of Shakespeare, Maupassant, and Chekhov is both perceptive and false. Doggedly holding to the history of literary criticism, Wellek yet asserts that Soviet Russia has solved the problem of the artist's alienation from the masses—"at the expense of both the religious values dear to Tolstoy and the aesthetic subtleties he condemned" (291). But Robert W. Simmons, for one, asks for demonstration.[16]

XII   German Criticism: From Hettner to Nietzsche

German literary criticism flourished during this time in the form of literary historiography, literary biography, and technical poetics. Because of its successful combination of narration, characterization, and criticism, Wellek admires the six-volume *Literary History of the Eighteenth Century* (1856–70) of Hermann Hettner (1821–82), particularly the volumes on the German Enlightenment. Wellek interestingly relates this inflexible liberal's *History* to his early work. Though Hettner lacks evocative power and understanding of allegory and symbolism, Wellek yet judges Hettner's *History*, all in all, superior to Taine's.

Compared to Hettner, William Scherer (1841–86) is naive, his taste a hodgepodge of classical, realistic, and academic. Wellek treats the positivist's scientific ideals and circumspect practices in source studies, analogues, parallels, and life models. Dazzled by the vision of comparative poetics, laws of history, and total deterministic explanation, Scherer in his unfinished *Poetik* (1888) reveals to Wellek a basic conflict, its roots in Romantic German philology.

Scherer's successor at the University of Berlin, the elegant official Erich Schmidt (1853–1903), wrote the monumental two-volume *Lessing* (1884, 1892) in a precious, allusive style. Another of Scherer's students, the witty but often absurd Richard Moritz Meyer (1860–1916), wrote a continuation of Scherer's *History* in *German Literature of the Nineteenth Century* (1900). Wellek's criticism is pertinent: "The reaction in the 20th century against the factualism, source and parallel hunting, biographical obsession, literary insensibility, and philosophical emptiness of academic scholarship found in Scherer and his school a symbol for a phenomenon that actually extended far beyond the few scholars directly associated with the man, and which had its analogues all over the Western world, including the universities of the United States" (303).

The judicious rationalist Rudolf Haym (1821–1901) is the first master of the peculiarly German literary biography: the evolutionary study of an author's personality and his work. Wellek remarks on Haym's admirable, sometimes reductive, biographies of Wilhelm von Humboldt, Hegel, Herder, and others. Like Hettner, Haym spurned positivism, relativism, Romanticism, and speculative philosophy by returning to the "historical school," to Goethe, to Kant, to Herder.

Of later nineteenth-century critics who focus on single genres—who "think as craftsmen, as practitioners who want to formulate the principles and even tricks of their trade" (305)—Wellek treats three. The dramatist Otto Ludwig (1813–65) left a mass of fragments on dramatic theory, Shakespeare, Schiller, and Hebbel. His contradictory yet appealing *Shakespearestudien* (1874) develops motifs from Lessing, Vischer, and Gervinus. Wellek first discusses Ludwig on inspiration, tragedy and Shakespeare, and then relates Ludwig's emphasis on psychological motivation, poetical realism, and logical composition to his reflections on the novel. Though Ludwig sees *Technik des Dramas* (1863) of the Aristotelian Gustav Freytag (1816–95) as properly superficial, Wellek notes that the conception in Freytag's modernized *Poetics* is close to Ludwig's—minus Freytag's Philistine optimism. More original are the pre-Jamesian reflections on the objective novel in *Contribution to Theory and Technique of the Novel* (1883) by the popular writer Friedrich Spielhagen (1829–1911). But Wellek rightly thinks that Spielhagen—like Flaubert and James—pushes the novel too far toward drama, for "even the capricious digressions of Sterne do not damage the objective fictive existence of Uncle Toby or Walter Shandy" (310).

Wellek spotlights a few more Germans. The attractive cosmopolitan Karl Hillebrand (1829–84) receives a marrowy biographical-bibliographical invoice, the esteem for his portraits tempered by inevitable specimens of his misjudgments. The optimistic Theodor Fontane (1819–98) at first welcomed Naturalism and long defended Realism, but Wellek sees as the key to Fontane's criticism "transfiguration," a term drawn from Classical aesthetics. Bringing to mind the bromides of German Naturalism, Wellek yet indicates the niceties of some theatrical discussion, particularly the pro-Naturalist criticism of Otto Brahm (1851–1912).

Agents of anti-Naturalism in the *History* are the psychiatrist Max Nordau (1849–1923) and the Marxist Franz Mehring (1846–1916). Wellek describes Nordau's *Degeneration* (1892), the sweeping diagnostic attack on modern literature, as decadent, neurotic, mad; siding with none of the contemporary Communist disputants regarding the "deviation" or "correctness" of the classical but class-minded Mehring, Wellek focuses on the influential *Lessing-Legende* (1893), which "shows, in germ, the fatal consequences of economic materialism when applied to imaginative literature or aesthetic ideas" (318).

A special chapter on the prolific and erudite Wilhelm Dilthey (1833–1911) makes him the central figure in the history of hermeneutics and raises again the problem of historical relativism. Wellek sees him in two fairly independent roles: historian of German literature and propounder of psychological poetics. Among Dilthey's fourteen large volumes, Wellek takes up *Die Einbildungskraft des Dichters* (1887), *Das Erlebnis und die Dichtung* (1905), and other works. He poses sharp queries about one of Dilthey's key terms, *Erlebnis*—that intense psychic experience fusing intellect, will, and feeling—the experience supposedly underlying all genuine poetry. For Wellek, art is grounded in tradition, technique, craft; for Dilthey, art is expression of experience, symbolization of inner states. Dilthey's six "circles of feeling" is for Wellek cloudy, obscuring the problem of mental images or feelings passing into a linguistic construct. Equally obscure is Dilthey's "inner form" derived from German Romantic aesthetics.

As in *Theory of Literature*, Wellek notes Dilthey's labors to distinguish between historical and scientific methodology and his efforts to identify literature with three philosophical world-views: positivism (Hobbes, Stendhal), objective idealism (Hegel, Goethe), dualistic idealism (Kant, Schiller). In practice, however, Dilthey seems to Wellek to have surrendered neither to relativism nor to historicism, but to have opted for objective idealism and Schleiermacher's hermeneutic circle. Seeing the problem of unity in formalistic terms, Wellek sympathetically reveals Dilthey's late repudiation of his psychologistic conception, his relevant last efforts to detach the imaginative nexus from the occasion, to study the artwork as meaning, structure, and value.

By reading imaginatively and contextually the perturbed but influential criticism of Friedrich Nietzsche (1844–1900), Wellek discerns a coherent theory of tragedy and literary history. Unlike most historians, Wellek relates the well-known Apollonian-Dionysiac dichotomy in *Birth of Tragedy* (1872) first to the philosopher's metaphysics of the universe as aesthetic phenomenon and then to his intricate historical scheme. To throw further light on Nietzsche's concept of tragedy as exaltation of life in spite of its horror, Wellek refers to other works and outlines the similarities and dissimilarities between Nietzsche's ideas and early sources, Schopenhauer and Wagner. Still, Nietzsche's explanation of the origin of tragedy from the Dionysiac chorus remains as obscure to Wellek as Nietzsche's assertion of the origin of poetry from music. Wellek brings out four motifs: the early theory of tragedy, the criticism of decadence and historicism, the vitalistic aesthetics, and the defense of Classicism. Wellek shows how Nietzsche—after disillusionment with Schopenhauer, Wagner, art, the artist, and himself—returned from nihilism to vitalistic aesthetics. Nietzsche glorified the true artist and defined art as not disinterested contemplation, but as transfigured sensuality, Dionysiac intoxication, ecstatic suffering, willed illusion—as a reality-violating service to life. "Something like romantic irony, even divine buffoonery," says Wellek, "is Nietzsche's ideal" (346). Thus Wellek sees Nietzsche's idolization of European Classicism as contrived, his admiration for French aphoristic prose seeming greater than his praise of Classical poetry and drama. Nietzsche attacks historicism and naturalism, false aestheticism and false philology, but often applauds writers without giving reasons. However forcefully Nietzsche reconciled the Dionysiac and the Classical in his own mind, Wellek the theorist remains unsatisfied.

XIII   *Danish Criticism: Brandes*

The chapter on Georg Brandes (1842–1927) apparently has satisfied Danish specialists. Discussing the conflicts surrounding "the lonely Dane," Wellek takes seriously Brandes's six-volume *Main Currents of Nineteenth-Century Literature* (1872–90). Wellek outlines Brandes's liberalism, but sees him as more than a "mere ideologist." Still, Brandes's judgments tend to be predictable. Wellek shows how, with respect to Romanticism, Brandes attacks the Germans, distorts the English, and praises the French. As a Jewish liberal, Brandes fervently analyzed and admired Heine. Before the Dane turned to positivism by way of Taine and to portraiture by way of Sainte-Beuve, he wrote books on aesthetics inspired by Hegel and Vischer.

Wellek sees Brandes at his best, however, as a critic of Danish literature. Unfortunately, his influential *Søren Kierkegaard* (1877) fumbles with his subject's religion and philosophy, if not with his anti-clericalism and individualism. As a cultural intermediary, Brandes promoted Ibsen from the start, preferring his realism to his symbolism. Wellek discusses Brandes's strong and weak judgments on Nietzsche, whose correspondence with him turned the Dane from optimistic liberalism to hero worship and literary biography. In his neglected *William Shakespeare* (1895–96), Brandes confuses ethical development with aesthetic criteria—as when he assumes that the sentiments of Shakespeare and Hamlet are identical. Brandes's late *Goethe* (1914–15) and *Voltaire* (1916–17) are perceptive, but Wellek finds Brandes more interested in the men than in their books.

XIV   *English Criticism: Swinburne to Shaw*

In "The English Aesthetic Movement," Wellek cautions that "aestheticism" often is merely "the defense of the artist against the arrogant moral pretentions of his critics" (371). After sketching the aesthetics of the Pre-Raphaelite Brotherhood, Wellek asserts that in England Algernon Swinburne (1837–1909) alone propounded the doctrine of "art for art's sake," albeit not always unequivocally. To reveal the creed at its purest, Wellek discusses Swinburne's satisfyingly concrete *William Blake* (1868). Swinburne indeed reacted excessively against the moralists, but he also acknowledged organic unity, failing at times, however, to apply it. From Wellek's vantage, Swinburne over-relied on his instincts, felt pleasure in uncritical extremes: superlative praise for Milton, Hugo, and Shelley—vituperation for Euripides, Heine, and Emerson.

Wellek himself advocates comparison and ranking, but he objects to Swinburne's arbitrariness: his quibbling and nonaesthetic attack on Byron, his exaltation of Shelley above Coleridge and far above Wordsworth and Keats. Even after applying the standard of Swinburne's own "pure poetry" (thrilling images and sound), Wellek finds the poet's judgments groundless. Swinburne exalted the Elizabethan dramatists; but Wellek finds *A Study in Shakespeare* (1880) "comparatively sober and disappointingly unoriginal" (379). Exhibiting Swinburne's elaborate failures, Wellek yet awakens us to the aesthetic *core* of Swinburne's criticism—more dense, tough, and discriminating than that of his English models, Leigh Hunt and Charles Lamb.

Such famous metaphorical passages as those on the *Mona Lisa* and the "hard, gemlike flame" Wellek cites as unrepresentative of the method and philosophy of Walter Pater (1839–94). Pleasurable impressionism is for Pater a prerequisite for penetrating art, for formulating the artist's "motive." Thus Wellek, freeing Pater from prejudices, illustrates the finesse of his traditional methods (historical, evocative, evaluative) by turning to his sympathetic essay on

Wordsworth in *Appreciations* (1889). Wellek suggests the subtleties and the flaws in Pater's essays on Shakespeare, Browne, Coleridge, Lamb, Morris, and Rossetti. In his discussion of *The Renaissance* (1873), Wellek draws our attention to curious exclusions and sources, as well as to portions which Pater later incorporated in his fiction. "Obviously," points out Wellek, "one must not treat Pater's fiction precisely as criticism, but it is difficult not to touch on it, as whole chapters of *Marius the Epicurean* and *Gaston de Latour* are concerned with works of literature . . ." (386–87).

Pater's taste is late Romantic, as Wellek sees it, but Pater's own use of the term seems too inclusive to be useful. His "aesthetic hedonism" is seen as a form of empiricism and sensationalism, his high poetry as lyrical, emotional, intense—a sincere particularization of the moment. Wellek thoroughly traces the subtle twists and turns of Pater's well-known essay "On Style" (1889). As religious convert, Pater recants his earlier insight into the unity of form and content. Wellek brilliantly decides that in Pater's work—in his oscillations on historicism and relativism, atmosphere and design, the Time-Spirit and the individual—nineteenth-century Alexandrian eclecticism and cultish Beauty intertwine.

The historian next corrects the view that John Addington Symonds (1840–93) is a follower of Pater. In a style evocative but essentially rational, Symonds's histories expound a cosmic evolutionism inspired by Hegel, Wordsworth, Goethe, and Whitman. Wellek outlines the birth-adolescence-maturity-decline-death scheme underlying Symonds's view of art: nonevolutionary patterns as in Roman art, Ben Jonson, the novel, and Victorian poetry are "hybrids." In the face of evolutionary inevitability, Symonds still calls for judicial criticism—though Wellek notes that Symonds's Baroque "decadence" is really a matter of taste, not fact.

Symonds sees the true critic as a combination of absolutist judge, impressionistic showman, and scientific historian—a theory Wellek deems excellent. He discusses Symonds's appreciative *Shelley* (1878) and *Walt Whitman* (1893) as peripheral to his seven-volume *The Renaissance in Italy* (1875–86). As in his early *Introduction to the Study of Dante* (1872), Symonds's *Renaissance* compiles too much elementary information; skillfully written, it yet lacks De Sanctis's critical focus and boldness. These defects, Wellek judges, are not found in Symonds's *Shakespeare's Predecessors in the English Drama* (1884), "one of the few great achievements of English literary historiography in the 19th century" (407).

Unwilling to confuse art and sexual deviation, Wellek demurs
regarding the confession of Oscar Wilde (1856–1900) as a martyr of
aestheticism. But Wellek sees Wilde as the representative of the
English aesthetic movement—witty, a propagandist with sources in
Arnold, Swinburne, Gautier, Poe, Baudelaire, and especially Pater.
Within the glittering prose of the dialogues and essays in *Intentions*
(1890), Wellek discerns critical insight. But Wilde flippantly shifts
between panaestheticism, decorative formalism, and the autonomy
of art. Though the dandified Wilde exotically preached life for art's
sake, Wellek's penetrating essay reveals a tough-minded Hegelian
dialectics of art: the union of content and form, technique and personality, subjective and objective, conscious and unconscious. Wellek naturally finds Wilde's highly subjective arguments for creative
criticism in "The Critic as Artist" (1890) untenable. Still, Wellek can
support ideas like critical fidelity, the artwork's inexhaustibility,
disdain for false objectivity. But what makes Oscar Wilde the quintessential figure of English aestheticism for Wellek is "precisely the
way Wilde juggled his terms, advanced and retreated from sense
to nonsense, from paradox to commonplace" (415).

Of particular interest is Wellek's generous treatment of his obvious rival—bookish George Saintsbury (1845–1933), author of the
first universal history of criticism and by far the most influential
academic literary historian and critic of the early twentieth century.
Wellek cites the relevant works in French, English, and general
literature—a part of what in a total collection would make perhaps
a hundred volumes. But underlying this variety and scope, Wellek
detects only a few simple principles. In poetry, Saintsbury is a
radical formalist who seeks the atomistic but pleasurable "poetic
moment," a mysterious conjunction of image, phrase, and sound
leading to critical impressionism. "The dichotomy between variable
form and monotonous content necessarily stunts his insight into the
world of intellect and thought and his interest in intellectual history"
(418).

In Saintsbury's three-volume *History of Criticism and Literary
Taste in Europe* (1901–1904) Wellek sees valuable mapmaking but
little genuine criticism, particularly of Russian, German, and Italian
literary study. In justice, however, Wellek finds Saintsbury at times
objecting to caprice, advising the reader to correct or check his
impressions through a catholicity of knowledge—leading to tolerance, comparison, appreciation, judging, and ranking. Wellek
sharply notes, however, Saintsbury's national prejudices regarding

European Realism and Naturalism, as well as his unconventional
taste for Baudelaire and Donne. Without recourse to announced
aesthetics, Saintsbury in practice, says Wellek, does refer to literary
theory and history. But mainly Wellek objects to Saintsbury's hazy
notions and criteria. *The History of English Prosody* (1906–10) and
The History of Prose Rhythm (1912), for example, have vague prem-
ises and much extraneous matter. Wellek finds *The History of the
French Novel* (1917–19) best because Saintsbury views the novel
not as momentary pleasure but mainly as a criticism of life. But
even here Wellek finds the critical tools of plot, character, description, and dialogue too restrictive. "The image of a fatherly authority,
of an omniscient reader, a somewhat crotchety but amiable con-
noisseur, and a John Bullish, no-nonsense Englishman is established" (426). Saintsbury's moralistic asides and personalized
whimsicalities give him a place among the English essayists.

In spite of his professed break with tradition, the witty George
Bernard Shaw (1856–1950) belongs for Wellek "to the Victorian
propounders of realism, common sense, and optimism, and the
enemies of romanticism and pessimism" (429). Wellek finds *The
Quintessence of Ibsenism* (1891) disappointing literary criticism, for
Shaw seems to be describing his own plays. Wellek briefly analyzes
Shaw's uncongenial rationalism, particularly his Shakespeare criticism, in the light of simple Shavian standards: Is the play like real
life? Does it convey sensible, progressive ideas? Wellek naturally
sees Shaw's brand of enlightenment as arid, as insensitive to man's
inner life, to the essence of poetry and art.

XV   French Criticism: Baudelaire and Mallarmé

In his final chapter, on the French symbolists, Wellek puts Baudelaire into the Romantic aesthetic tradition, touches briefly on
Rimbaud, and concludes with Mallarmé's negative aesthetics—his
contrast to Zola and Tolstoy, The wavering theory of correspond-
ences and universal analogy of Charles Baudelaire (1821–67) leads
to his rejection of photographic realism. He conceives of the imagination as throwing supernatural light on the natural darkness of
things, as transforming nature, and thereby creating a thoroughly
human cosmos.

Though Baudelaire's poetry transmitted the symbol to modern
poetry, Wellek points out that the terms "symbol" and "myth" are
not prominent in Baudelaire's criticism. Of his brother Albert's many

articles in German dealing with synesthesia, Wellek cites three in his Bibliography (627) and clarifies Baudelaire's interest in the phenomenon as a rhetoric of analogizing. "The false idea thàt this single device is central to symbolism and its interpretation as a clinical trait of the poets have made symbolism suspect as decadent and pathological" (445). Compared to Rimbaud's bravado, says Wellek, Baudelaire's literary criticism is a model of sobriety. Still, however significant Baudelaire's discovery of his cherished Poe, Wellek thinks that the Frenchman overrated the American's poetry and intellect. Understanding Baudelaire's admiration and despair of Hugo, Wellek thinks him blind to Gautier's limitations. Though he deems Baudelaire's criticism of the novel superior to his criticism of poetry, Wellek cites only Baudelaire's sympathetic review of *Madame Bovary* as first-rate. Clearly, Wellek finds Baudelaire's theory and practice of literary criticism inferior to his theory and practice of art criticism.

Wellek sees the ideal beauty of Stéphane Mallarmé (1842–98) as more icy than Poe's, the ideal imagination as more remote from reality than Baudelaire's. Quoting from essays in *Divagations* (1897) and from letters and interviews, Wellek cogently explains Mallarmé's discontent with ordinary language, his attempts to create a separate poetic diction, language as magic, words as things. Wellek outlines Mallarmé's views on sound and sense, the rhythm of the Idea, and the graphic qualities of printed *vers libre* and the book's format.

Wellek indicates that Mallarmé later envisioned a collective art, but that in the end only a solitary, exclusive art was possible for him: the planned dream of a divine, intricate, twenty-volume organism—"The Book"—suspended over the Void, the silent Goddess Nothingness. In Mallarmé, poetry absorbs all reality and becomes the only reality; in Zola and Tolstoy and many others, art is identification with life and becomes superfluous and finally useless. "Clearly," says Wellek, closing the fourth volume of his great history and opening a vista onto future volumes, "the task of a new era would be a reassertion of the balance: a recognition of the independent autonomy of art but also its meaningful relation to the reality of nature, man, and society" (463).

XVI   History of Criticism *(V and VI)*

Ambitious readers will find in various journals and collections most chapters and sections—in early or final versions—of what will be the fifth and sixth volumes of René Wellek's *History* (see Notes and References and Selected Bibliography). The English-American volume will open with a chapter on Symbolism, mainly on W. B. Yeats, with shorter sections on Arthur Symons and George Moore. Next will come a chapter on A. C. Bradley in the idealist tradition. A long discussion of university studies and academic critics will follow, with accounts of Walter Raleigh, Arthur Quiller-Couch, Oliver Elton, W. P. Ker, Herbert Grierson, and H. W. Garrod. Wellek then will take up the Bloomsbury group: Clive Bell, Roger Fry, and especially Virginia Woolf. Shorter sections on Lytton Strachey, E. M. Forster, and Desmond MacCarthy will follow. Under New Romantics, Wellek plans to discuss the historical importance of John Middleton Murry and the oddly exalted position of D. H. Lawrence. Also planned are sections on G. Wilson Knight and possibly Herbert Read. Next come the Innovators—the contradictory T. E. Hulme, the erratic Ezra Pound, and the bifurcated T. S. Eliot. I. A. Richards's psychology will be rejected, his practical criticism accepted. Except for the later criticism, F. R. Leavis, too, will be treated sympathetically. Discussions on William Empson, F. W. Bateson, and possibly Wyndham Lewis will follow.

　　Criticism in America will begin with the New Humanists, mainly Paul Elmer More and Irving Babbitt. Next will come the New Aestheticism of James Huneker, Joel Spingarn, and George Santayana, followed by the New Nationalism of H. L. Mencken and Van Wyck Brooks. Wellek will devote a long chapter to Edmund Wilson as a critical middleman. The New Criticism will be emphasized, with chapters on Allen Tate, John Crowe Ransom, Cleanth Brooks, R. P. Blackmur, Kenneth Burke, Yvor Winters, and William K. Wimsatt, Jr. Sections on the Chicago Aristotelians and the Marxists of the 1930s will come next, with chapters on Lionel Trilling and F. O. Matthiessen closing the fifth volume. Wellek, in passing, comments on critics like Northrop Frye, Leslie Fiedler, Ihab Hassan, and Harold Bloom; but only critics whose *important first books* were published *before 1950* can be discussed fully.

　　The sixth volume will begin with Benedetto Croce, his followers, and such Italian critics as Mario Praz, Emilio Cecchi, and Cesare Pavese. Next come the many French critics, among them Albert Thibaudet, Charles Du Bos, Paul Valéry, Jean Paul Sartre, Albert Béguin, and George Poulet. Among the Germans, Wellek will treat Friedrich Gundolf, Max Kommerell, E. R. Curtius, Leo Spitzer,

Erich Auerbach, and Walter Benjamin. Long ago, of course, Wellek began writing about the Russian Formalists and the Czech Structuralists: attention naturally will be given to Jan Mukařovský, F. X. Šalda, and the Pole, Roman Ingarden. There will be a chapter on the Hungarian Marxist Georg Lukács. Finally, Wellek will discuss the Spaniard Ortega y Gasset, and possibly Dámaso Alonso, who wrote the preface to *Theoria literaria* (Spanish translation, 1953).

"Some work of noble note may yet be done."

CHAPTER 7

Critic of Critics

R ENÉ Wellek's life as a professor, theorist, historian, critic, and editor coincides with the rapid expansion of criticism and scholarship in America and Europe. Clearly, he has contributed enormously to this expansion—and to the Great Debate, to what W. B. Gallie calls "essentially contested concepts." One associates *Theory of Literature* with such reforming American statements as George Santayana's *Sense of Beauty* (1896), Joel Spingarn's *New Criticism* (1911), T. S. Eliot's "Tradition and the Individual Talent" (1919), Cleanth Brooks and Robert Penn Warren's *Understanding Poetry* (1938), and John Crowe Ransom's *New Criticism* (1941). With other literary scholars in the twentieth-century critical vanguard, René Wellek and Austin Warren helped loosen the academic stranglehold of nineteenth-century positivism. E. D. Hirsch, Jr., commenting recently on the vigorous polemics between the Chicago and the New Haven critics, observes: "No matter if Aristotle or if Coleridge was taken to be the true prophet of the revolution, its goal was conceived by both parties to be the criticism of literature as literature."[1]

One must remember, however, that while René Wellek called for intense critical exploration of the text, he never abandoned the historical method embodied in his *Kant in England* and *The Rise of English Literary History*. His synthesis of theory, criticism, and history reflects a passionate dedication to literary studies as a humane discipline, its standards derived not from "personal" taste or "impersonal science," but from the norms of history. For Wellek, the literary work is no simple verbal construct and no mere reflection of society: it is a phenomenological aesthetic object. Thus criticism means concern for values and qualities. Understanding—adequate analysis, interpretation, and evaluation—requires theory. Adequate theory requires a history of criticism. And adequate history requires an international perspective.

Envisioning the distant ideal of universal literary history and scholarship, Wellek in *A History of Modern Criticism* richly contributes to what Aldo Scaglione calls "an ecumenical republic of letters."[2] At least to the chief critical nations in the Western tradition, Wellek offers a splendid view of the other nations. His historical imagination and critical intelligence vivify not only high-ranking and familiar critics, but also the unfashionable, the forgotten, the unknown. His work enlarges one's awareness of criticism as a discipline, of modern literary theory as growing out of the past, of German innovation in shaping the New Criticism, and of the New Criticism in relation to wider European currents. Though Wellek failed to devise an "evolutionary" scheme, *Theory of Literature* informs *A History of Modern Criticism*. Formed out of critical chaos, so to speak, the coherent *Theory* reenters that chaos, imparting to a substantial time sequence a reasonable unity, making the diverse episodes of the critical epic—the *History*—hang together.

The twentieth-century revolt against positivism and impressionism generated not only critics and critics of critics, but critics of critics of critics. To Arthur Mizener, *Theory of Literature* represented both a beginning and a summing up, "a kind of *summa*."[3] New developments and the book's wide acceptance today diminish difficulties once considered "novel." Still, some critics point to what they take to be Wellek's inordinate appetite for theory. They object also to what they see as "pigeonholing." But Wellek's sophisticated categories—even the emphatic "extrinsic" and "intrinsic" approaches—are neither pedantic nor ossified. W. K. Wimsatt early pointed out that they are "far from the neat philological categories and formal examples of traditional manuals."[4] But even Wellek's repetitions, remarks Scaglione, are various and fresh, "seldom monotonous or otiose."[5]

To characterize *the* critic of critics, reviewers have drawn images from such areas as sports, medicine, law, and politics. Amusingly enough, René Wellek has been likened to a universal umpire, to an observer on a mountaintop, to an intellectual physician, to a firm but kindly traffic policeman, to a tireless United Nations man going around ascertaining justice. For all his decisiveness and outspokenness, however, Wellek follows the sane middle path. He is never doctrinaire or rancorous. "If he finds no critic beyond all censure," observes Walter J. Ong, "he also finds even in the very worst at least some little point worth commendation."[6] Even his trenchant and balanced book reviews—for which he seems often to turn over many other books—exemplify the art and craft of criticism in a small compass.

"Massive," "omnivorous," "staggering," "enviable," "faultless," "unnerving," "forbidding" are a few of the more colorful adjectives applied to René Wellek's erudition. So awesome, in fact is his "Pan-European" learning—and so imperative apparently the need to believe in human fallibility—that one seems to hear mollifying sighs from reviewers who spot in Wellek's astonishing scholarship a name off by a letter, a date off by a year. With the resources of Western literary thought at his command, he naturally seems at times esoteric. But he himself thinks of erudition in the service of evaluation. He would even like to take Roger Sales's remark in *Hudson Review* (that Wellek's erudition has "blown competition" from the field of criticism) as a compliment, for "I cannot think of ignorance as a merit."[7]

When influence and authority in scholarship after World War II passed to the United States, many European scholars foresaw American learning resembling American industry. Indeed, the brightly packaged efficiency of American literary scholarship has never been questioned. But always Wellek's influence toward a coherent, superpersonal, humanistic tradition has been in the direction of excellence. Wellek at Yale was always there, Geoffrey Hartman recalls, to set the standard. "Most Americans who aspire to criticism have learned from him," wrote Monroe K. Spears, "and many of us feel that literary studies would be in a healthier condition if we had learned more."[8]

In spite of the doubting philologists and historians, the analytical influence of Wellek and Warren's *Theory of Literature* has been profound. Correctly, Howard Mumford Jones surmised that it would be "in every learned library."[9] George Whicher predicted that it would "nourish scholars for a generation to come and change the direction of education with beneficial results."[10] Thirty years after the first publication of *Theory*, Russian and Chinese translations join the score of others, ready to nourish another generation of literary scholars. Similarly, Mark Schorer declared that *A History of Modern Criticism* would be the "standard reference for decades to come."[11] Specialists and nonspecialists alike seem inspired by Wellek to study, to defend, to refute. As the Chinese go to the Great Wall for stones, so scholars come to Wellek for concepts.

What makes his influence so wholesome is that over the years he has reminded his students and his readers—Monroe Spears again—

that our vision of truth is only partial, that our assumptions are limited, that consensus might be fruitful.[12] René Wellek has asserted: "Men can correct their biases, criticize their presuppositions, rise above their temporal and local limitations, aim at objectivity, arrive at some knowledge and truth."[13] In pursuing knowledge and truth in Europe and America, he has struggled to maintain his critical independence and integrity. For himself, he has gained many honors; for his adopted homeland, much prestige. "The world may be dark and mysterious,"—so writes this American from Central Europe—"but it is surely not completely unintelligible."[14] Whatever else is obscure, clearly the world's greatest living historian of literary criticism is himself a signal part of that history.

Notes and References

Chapter One

1. *World Authors: 1950–1970,* ed. John Wakeman (New York: H. W. Wilson, 1975), p. 1525.
2. "An *Arion* Questionnaire," *Arion* 3 (Winter 1964): 89.
3. "Twenty Years of Czech Literature: 1918–1938," *Essays on Czech Literature* (The Hague: Mouton, 1963), p. 35.
4. "Germans and Czechs in Bohemia," ibid., p. 78.
5. "The Literary Criticism of Friedrich Gundolf," *Contemporary Literature* 9 (Summer 1968): 395.
6. "Vilém Mathesius (1882–1945): Founder of the Prague Linguistic Circle," *Sound, Sign and Meaning,* ed. L. Matějka (Ann Arbor: University of Michigan Press, 1976), p. 14.
7. Ibid.
8. "Okleštěný Shakespeare," *Kritika* 1 (1924): 243–45.
9. "On two occasions when I called on Mr. More in Princeton in 1929, he lent me, I remember, the *Sermons* of John Smith and *The Candle of the Lord* by Nathaniel Calderwell." Wellek, "Irving Babbitt, Paul More, and Transcendentalism," *Transcendentalism and Its Legacy,* ed. Myron Simon and T. H. Parsons (Ann Arbor: University of Michigan Press, 1966), p. 201.
10. "Vilém Mathesius," p. 13. The published inaugural lecture is in *Listy pro umění a kritiku* 1 (1933): 66–71.
11. *Charisteria Guilelmo Mathesio . . . Oblata* (Prague: Charles University, 1932), pp. 130–34.
12. "Literary Criticism and Philosophy," *Scrutiny* 5 (March 1937): 375–83.
13. *Scrutiny* 6 (June 1937): 59–70.
14. *Scrutiny* 6 (September 1937): 195–96.
15. According to Calvin S. Brown, in *Comparative Literature* 17 (Spring 1965): 162, "It is a great advantage to be able by firsthand knowledge to relate the ideas of the Prague Circle and the Russian Formalists to the concepts of Western European scholarship."
16. "Collaborating with Austin Warren on *Theory of Literature,*" *Teacher and Critic: Essays by and about Austin Warren,* ed. Myron Simon and Harvey Gross (Los Angeles: The Plantin Press, 1976), p. 73.
17. "Comparative Literature at Yale," *Ventures Magazine* 10 (Spring 1970): 24–32.
18. Spanish, Japanese, Italian, German, Korean, Portuguese, Danish,

Serbo-Croat, Greek, Swedish, Hebrew, Romanian, Finnish, Hindi, Norwegian, Polish, French, Hungarian, Dutch, Arabic, Russian, Chinese.

19. Wellek and Austin Warren, *Theory of Literature*, 3rd rev. ed. (New York: Harcourt, Brace, 1962), p. 27.

20. See "The Concept of Romanticism in Literary History," *Comparative Literature* 1 (Winter 1949): 1–23; (Spring 1949): 147–72, and Lovejoy, "On the Discrimination of Romanticisms," *PMLA* 29 (June 1924): 229–53.

21. *Saturday Review*, July 16, 1955, p. 25.

22. *Journal of Aesthetics and Art Criticism* 22 (Spring 1964): 354.

23. *Modern Language Quarterly* 26 (June 1965): 354.

24. Ronald Hafter, *Dalhousie Review* 46 (Autumn 1966): 403.

25. *British Journal of Aesthetics* 2 (Spring 1971): 205.

26. 12 (Fall 1960): 376–77.

27. May 28, 1947, p. 6.

28. *A History of Modern Criticism: 1750–1950*, 2 (New Haven: Yale University Press, 1955), p. 293. Subsequently identified as *History*.

29. *History*, 3 (New Haven: Yale University Press, 1965), p. 225.

30. *History*, 4 (New Haven: Yale University Press, 1965), p. 382.

31. *Concepts of Criticism*, edited with an Introduction by Stephen G. Nichols, Jr. (New Haven: Yale University Press, 1963), p. 202.

32. "Style in Literature, Closing Statement," *Style in Language*, ed. T. A. Sebeok (Cambridge, Massachusetts: Technology Press and John Wiley, 1960), p. 409.

33. *Discriminations: Further Concepts of Criticism* (New Haven and London: Yale University Press, 1970), p. 67.

34. Ibid., p. 92.

35. "Prospect and Retrospect," *Yale Review* 49 (Winter 1980): 301–12.

Chapter Two

1. Page references in text are to *Confrontations: Studies in the Intellectual and Literary Relations between Germany, England, and the United States during the Nineteenth Century* (Princeton, New Jersey: Princeton University Press, 1965).

2. *Mind* 41 (October 1932): 518.

3. Anon., *Modern Language Review* 29 (January 1934): 113.

4. *Mind* 41:518–21.

5. Page references in text are to *Immanuel Kant in England: 1793–1838* (Princeton, New Jersey: Princeton University Press, 1931).

6. "René Wellek," *Encyclopedia of World Literature in the Twentieth Century*, 4, ed. W. B. Fleischmann (New York: Ungar, 1975), p. 391.

7. *Journal of English and Germanic Philology* 32 (July 1933): 424.

8. Wellek published Robinson's translation of Savigny's manuscript "On the Present State of the German Universities," as "Ein unbekannter

Artikel Savignys über die deutschen Universitäten" in *Savigny-Stiftung für Rechtsgeschichte* 51 (Easter 1931): 529–37.
9. *Mind* 41:519.
10. 14 (July–September 1934): 372–76.
11. In *Co číst z literatur germánských posledních desíti let* (Prague: Fr. Borový, 1935), pp. 7–69.
12. See Bibliography, *Essays on Czech Literature*, pp. 13–15.
13. "The Literary Theories of F. W. Bateson," *Essays in Criticism* 29 (April 1979): 112–23.
14. "Cambridgská skupina literárnich teoretiku," *Slovo a slovesnost* 3 (1937): 108–21.
15. "Šklovského Teorie prózy," *Listy pro umění a kritiku* 2 (1934): 111–15.
16. "Mezinárodní kongres filosofický," ibid., pp. 257–66.
17. *Slavic and East European Journal*, Summer 1964, p. 206.
18. *Slavonic Review* 16 (1938): 481–84.
19. *Slavonic and East European Review* 43 (June 1965): 443.
20. May 21, 1964, p. 436.
21. 23 (1944): 186–89.
22. *Journal of English and Germanic Philology* 41 (January 1942): 115.
23. Page references in text are to *The Rise of English Literary History* (Chapel Hill: University of North Carolina Press, 1941).
24. *Modern Philology* 40 (May 1943): 361.
25. *Journal of English and German Philology* (41:115) cites Arundell Esdaile's *List of English Tales and Prose Romances* and Charles Gerring's *Notes on Printers and Booksellers*.
26. Ibid.
27. *Saturday Review of Literature*, July 12, 1941, p. 8.
28. *Philological Quarterly* 21 (April 1942): 196.
29. 37 (November 1965): 363.
30. *Comparative Literature* 18 (Spring 1966): 183.
31. *The Scholar-Critic* (London: Routledge and K. Paul, 1972), p. 53.

Chapter Three

1. *Germanic Review* 24 (December 1949): 304.
2. January 30, 1949, p. 14.
3. November 19, 1949, p. 34.
4. *Romance Philology* 11 (May 1958): 403.
5. *Antioch Review* 10 (March 1950): 147.
6. *Kenyon Review* 12 (Winter 1950): 165.
7. *Romance Philology* 11:401.
8. *Yale Review* 39 (Autumn 1949): 180.
9. *Scrutiny* 16 (September 1949): 262.
10. Ibid., p. 260.

162 RENÉ WELLEK

11. Page references in text are to *Theory of Literature,* 3rd rev. ed. (New York: Harcourt, Brace, 1962).

12. See "Stylistics, Poetics, and Criticism," *Discriminations,* pp. 327–43.

13. "Literature, Fiction, and Literariness," paper read at Innsbruck Congress of Comparative Literature, 1979.

14. "The Problem of Greatness in Writing Literary History," *English Institute Annual 1940* (New York: Columbia University Press, 1941), p. 113. Others have translated the term as "perspective realism" or "objective realism."

15. See "The Crisis of Comparative Literature," *Concepts,* pp. 282–95.

16. See Wellek's appreciative review of Erich Auerbach's *Mimesis* in *Kenyon Review* 16 (Spring 1954): 299–307.

17. Spencer, *Modern Language Review* 44 (October 1949): 321; *Scrutiny* 16:260.

18. *Partisan Review* 16 (March 1949): 321.

19. *Kenyon Review* 12:165; Howe, *Nation,* July 16, 1949, p. 64; Geismar, *New Republic,* April 11, 1949, p. 23.

20. M. B. Bern, reviewing Albert Wellek's *Witz-Lyrik-Sprache* (1970) in *Modern Language Review* 68 (April 1973): 463–64, points out the author's interest in theory of literature, his ability to combine psychological and literary experience, and his high degree of methodological awareness.

21. *Linguistics and Literary Theory* (New York: W. W. Norton, 1969), p. 189.

22. *Yale Review* 39:182.

23. *English Studies Today* 2 (1961): 73.

24. In, respectively, *Western Review* 12 (Autumn 1947): 52–54; *Modern Philology* 47 (August 1949): 39–45; and *Kenyon Review* 11 (Summer 1949): 500–506.

Chapter Four

1. Page references in text are to *Essays on Czech Literature* (The Hague: Mouton, 1963).

2. *Slavonic and East European Review* 43:445.

3. *Slavic and East European Journal,* Summer 1964, p. 206.

4. *Essays on Czech Literature,* p. 7.

5. In, respectively, *Czech Literature at the Crossroads of Europe* (Toronto: The Toronto Chapter of the Czechoslovak Society of Arts and Sciences in America, 1963) and *Czechoslovakia Past and Present,* 2, ed. M. Rechcígl, Jr. (The Hague: Mouton, 1969).

6. "Ritratti critici di contemporanei," *Belfagor* 24 (1969): 566–67, 574–75.

7. *College English* 24 (May 1963): 663.

8. Dimitri von Mohrenshildt, *Russian Review* 22 (January 1964): 82; Ralph E. Matlaw, *Slavic Review* 22 (September 1963): 595.

9. *Review of English Studies* 27 (November 1966): 443.
10. *Modern Language Journal* 49 (October 1965): 393.
11. *Modern Language Quarterly* 26:355.
12. *Modern Language Notes* 83 (April 1968): 497.
13. *History and Theory* 6 (1967): 80.
14. *Comparative Literature* 18:183.
15. References in text are to *Concepts of Criticism* (New Haven and London: Yale University Press, 1963).
16. *Library Journal* 95 (September 15, 1970): 2920.
17. *Comparative Literature Studies* 9 (September 1972): 331.
18. References in text are to *Discriminations: Further Concepts of Criticism* (New Haven and London: Yale University Press, 1970).
19. *Comparative Literature Studies* 9:331.
20. *Revue de littérature comparée* 41 (July-September 1971): 402.
21. *American Literature* 36 (March 1964): 111.
22. Watson, *The Study of Literature* (London: Allen Lane, 1969), pp. 37–39; Scaglione, *Romance Philology* 27 (February 1964): 692.
23. "On the Theory of Romanticism," *The Fate of Reading* (Chicago: University of Chicago Press, 1975), p. 277.
24. See *Comparative Literature: Method and Perspective*, ed. N. P. Stallknecht and H. Frenz (Carbondale: Southern Illinois University Press, 1961), p. 277.
25. *Modern Language Journal* 48 (April 1964): 252.
26. "Reflections on Professor Wellek's Concept of Realism," *Neophilologus* 46 (April 1942): 89.
27. "A Reply to E. B. Greenwood's Reflections," ibid., 46 (July 1962): 194–96.
28. *Comparative Literature Studies* 9:334.
29. In Sebeok, *Style in Language*, pp. 408–19.
30. "In the paper given at the Ottawa Congress of the International Comparative Literature Association, 'Science, Pseudo-Science, and Intuition in Recent Criticism,' I ridicule the text-grammar of Van Dijk as well as statistical methods." Letter to Martin Bucco, 22 September 1979.
31. Walter H. Clark, Jr., *Journal of Aesthetics and Art Criticism* 30 (Spring 1972): 389; E. N. Tigerstedt, *Studia Neophilologica* 43 (No. 2 1971): 599.
32. One imagines the multitude of tongues in the streets of the Hapsburg capital . . . Bruegel's *Tower of Babel* hanging in the Kunsthistorisches Museum.
33. *Yearbook of Comparative and General Literature*, 20 (Bloomington: Indiana University Press, 1971), 5–14.
34. For a marvelously compact survey—"Literary Criticism"—see Wellek, *Dictionary of the History of Ideas* (New York: Scribner's, 1973), pp. 596–607.
35. *Philological Quarterly* 21 (April 1942): 255. Reviews of other surveys

and compendia mentioned are in *Comparative Literature* 3 (Spring 1951): 185–86; (Fall 1951): 364–66; and 2 (Spring 1950): 182–84.

36. February 12, 1971, p. 181.

37. *New York Times Book Review*, October 13, 1963, p. 34. For an impressive traditional festschrift on the occasion of Wellek's sixty-fifth birthday, see *The Disciplines of Criticism*, ed. Peter Demetz, Thomas Greene, and Lowry Nelson, Jr. (New Haven and London: Yale University Press, 1968).

38. *Kenyon Review* 26 (Spring 1964): 417.

39. *Comparative Literature* 17 (Spring 1965): 161.

40. *Comparative Literature Studies* 1 ([June] 1964): 155.

41. *Studia Neophilologica* 43:599.

42. *Notes and Queries* N.S. 20 (August 1973): 315–16.

43. *Yale Review* 60 (Autumn 1970): 135.

44. *Dalhousie Review* 46:407.

45. *Notes and Queries* N.S. 13 (March 1966): 113.

46. *Modern Philology* 12 (February 1965): 243.

47. *Chicago Tribune Book World*, August 2, 1970, p. 7.

48. December 1970, p. 1369.

49. *Kenyon Review* 26:418.

50. *Spectator*, December 13, 1963, p. 799.

51. *Times Literary Supplement*, February 12, 1971, p. 181.

52. *British Journal of Aesthetics* 2 (Spring 1971): 204.

53. In *Giambattista Vico: An International Symposium*, ed. G. Tagliacozzo and H. V. White (Baltimore: The Johns Hopkins University Press, 1969), pp. 215–23.

54. In *Studies on Voltaire and the Eighteenth Century*, V, ed. T. Bestermann (Oxford: The Voltaire Foundation and the Taylor Institution, 1976), pp. 2265–84.

55. *Midway* 8 (June 1967): 49–56.

56. Letter to Martin Bucco, 22 September 1979.

57. *Times Literary Supplement*, July 26, 1963, p. 49.

58. *Sewanee Review* 68 (April-June 1960): 349–50.

59. *Modern Language Review* 69 (October 1974); xxi–xxxi; *Proceedings of the American Philosophic Society* 119 (October 15, 1979): 397–400.

60. From a letter to Martin Bucco, 22 September 1979.

61. Ibid.

62. *Journal of English and Germanic Philology* 123 (July 1974): 459–62.

63. *American Scholar* 42 (Winter 1972–73): 27–42.

64. Wellek, letter to Martin Bucco, 22 September 1979, in reference to Grant Webster's *Republic of Letters* (Baltimore: The Johns Hopkins University Press, 1979).

65. In *Geschichte: Ereignis und Erzählung*, ed. R. Kosseleck and W-D. Stempel (Munich: Wilhelm Fink Verlag, 1973), pp. 427–40.

66. *Yale Review* 39:182.

67. *Comparative Literature Studies* 9:335.

68. Watson, *Review of English Studies* 19 (February 1963): 96; Dono-ghue, *Encounter* 28 (June 1967): 84.

69. *American Scholar* 35 (Summer 1966): 550.

Chapter Five

1. *Library Journal* 80 (June 1, 1955): 1886.

2. *Yale Review* 39 (Autumn 1949): 149. Abrams's book *The Mirror and the Lamp* sometimes is viewed—mistakenly—as the model for the *History;* Wellek's first two volumes, however, were ready for publication—originally by Oxford Press—in 1953, before Oxford's publication of Abrams's book that same year.

3. July 15, 1955, p. 465.

4. *Partisan Review* 23 (Winter 1956): 124.

5. *Encyclopedia of World Literature*, 4, p. 391.

6. Wellek, "Literary Criticism and Philosophy," p. 376.

7. *Criticism* 9 (Spring 1967): 197.

8. "Reply to Bernard Weinberg's Review of My *History of Criticism*," *Journal of the History of Ideas* 30 (April-June 1969): 281.

9. *Journal of Aesthetics and Art Criticism* 14 (Winter 1966): 232.

10. *Dalhousie Review* 46:401.

11. *Saturday Review,* July 16, 1955, p. 24.

12. *Criticism* 9:197.

13. *Partisan Review* 23:126.

14. See, for example, Robert W. Simmons, *Slavic and East European Journal* 20 (Summer 1967): 223; Wasiolek, *Modern Philology* 65 (August 1967): 91; and Watson, *Review of English Studies* 19:96–98.

15. *New York Times Book Review,* January 2, 1966, p. 7.

16. Page references in text are to *A History of Modern Criticism: 1750–1950,* 1, *The Later Eighteenth Century* (New Haven: Yale University Press, 1955).

17. *New York Times Book Review,* July 10, 1955, p. 6.

18. *The Poetics of Reason* (New York: Random House, 1968), p. 111.

19. See Wellek's review of Vico's *Autobiography* in *Philological Quarterly* 24 (April 1945): 166–68.

20. Marks, *Yale Review* 60:135.

21. *Review of English Studies* 21 (August 1971): 386.

22. Page references in text are to *A History of Modern Criticism: 1750–1950,* 2, *The Romantic Age* (New Haven: Yale University Press, 1955).

23. *Criticism* 9:197.

24. *New York Times Book Review,* July 10, 1955, p. 6.

25. *Partisan Review* 23:124.

26. *PTL: A Journal of Descriptive Poetics and Theory of Literature* 3 (1977): 418–19.

27. *Western Review* 21 (Winter 1957): 153.

28. See, respectively, *Virginia Quarterly Review* 32 (Spring 1956): 310–15; *Romanische Forschungen* 67 (1955): 387–97; *Listener*, November 3, 1955, pp. 755–57. In his Preface (III, vi), Wellek indicates that he is not convinced by Auerbach's argument "that criticism is not a unified subject because of the number of possible problems, and crossings of problems, the extreme diversity of its presuppositions, aims and accents." This diversity—the topic of the *History*—is aimed at a single subject—literature.

Chapter Six

1. August 31,1967, p. 782.
2. *Encounter* 28:82.
3. *Essays in Criticism* 18 (January 1968): 86.
4. *Hudson Review* 19 (Summer 1966): 325–29.
5. Page references in text are to *A History of Modern Criticism: 1750–1950*, 3, *The Age of Transition* (New Haven: Yale University Press, 1965).
6. *Encounter* 28:82.
7. See *World Masterpieces*, ed. Maynard Mack, 3rd ed. (New York: W. W. Norton, 1973), pp. 750–51, for Wellek's interesting "Editor's Note" on the *Lucia di Lammermoor* episode.
8. Page references in text are to *A History of Modern Criticism: 1750–1950*, 4, *The Later Nineteenth Century* (New Haven: Yale University Press, 1965).
9. *Journal of the History of Ideas* 30 (January-March 1969): 131.
10. See also Wellek, "Crisis of Comparative Literature," *Concepts*, pp. 282–95; "The Name and Nature of Comparative Literature," *Discriminations*, pp. 1–36; and "Comparative Literature at Yale," *Ventures Magazine*, pp. 24–32.
11. See "Modern Czech Criticism and Literary Scholarship," *Essays on Czech Literature*, pp. 179–93.
12. *George Henry Lewes as Literary Critic* (Syracuse: University of Syracuse Press, 1963), p. 185.
13. *Victorian Studies* 10 (March 1967): 308.
14. Anon. [probably the editor], *American Literature* 38 (May 1966): 270.
15. *Modern Philology* 65:91.
16. *Slavic and East European Journal* 20:224.

Chapter Seven

1. "Privileged Criteria in Literary Evaluation," *Problems of Literary Evaluation (Yearbook of Comparative Literature)*, 2, ed. Joseph P. Strelka

(University Park and London: Pennsylvania State University Press, 1969), p. 25.
2. *Romance Philology* 27:690.
3. *Furioso* 4 (Summer 1949): 87.
4. *Yale Review* 39:180-81.
5. *Romance Philology* 27:695.
6. *Yale Review* 55 (June 1966): 587.
7. Letter to Martin Bucco, 22 September 1979.
8. *Sewanee Review* 72 (Spring 1964): 321.
9. *Saturday Review*, April 30, 1949, p. 12.
10. *New York Herald Tribune Book Review*, March 27, 1949, p. 14.
11. *New York Times Book Review*, July 10, 1955, p. 6.
12. *Sewanee Review* 72:321-22.
13. "Literary Theory, Criticism, and History," *Concepts*, p. 4.
14. Ibid.

Selected Bibliography

PRIMARY SOURCES

René Wellek bibliographies from 1924 to 1969 (books, contributions to books, articles, reviews, miscellaneous) appear in *Essays on Czech Literature,* pp. 11–16; *Concepts of Criticism,* pp. 365–78; and *Discriminations,* pp. 361–68. The following highly selected bibliography lists his books—but not the many translations. It also includes Wellek's important uncollected articles, but not his many book reviews. Of particular value are listings of some early essays and many published between 1970–79 which will be incorporated into the fifth and sixth volumes of his *History of Modern Criticism.* René Wellek's large personal library of literary criticism will be transferred in stages to the University of California, Irvine.

1. Books

Concepts of Criticism. Edited with an Introduction by Stephen G. Nichols, Jr. New Haven and London: Yale University Press, 1963.
Confrontations: Studies in the Intellectual and Literary Relations between Germany, England, and the United States during the Nineteenth Century. Princeton: Princeton University Press, 1965.
Discriminations: Further Concepts of Criticism. New Haven and London: Yale University Press, 1970.
Essays on Czech Literature. Introduction by Peter Demetz. The Hague: Mouton, 1963.
A History of Modern Criticism: 1750–1950, 1, The Later Eighteenth Century. New Haven: Yale University Press, 1955.
A History of Modern Criticism: 1750–1950, 2, *The Romantic Age.* New Haven: Yale University Press, 1955.
A History of Modern Criticism: 1750–1950, 3, *The Age of Transition.* New Haven: Yale University Press, 1965; London: Jonathan Cape, 1966.
A History of Modern Criticism: 1750–1950, 4, *The Later Nineteenth Century.* New Haven: Yale University Press, 1965; London: Jonathan Cape, 1966.
Immanuel Kant in England: 1793–1838. Princeton: Princeton University Press, 1931.
The Literary Theory and Aesthetics of the Prague School. Michigan Slavic Contributions. Edited by Ladislaw Matějka. Ann Arbor: University of Michigan, 1969.
The Rise of English Literary History. Chapel Hill: University of North

Carolina Press, 1941. New ed. with "Preface to the Paperback." New York: McGraw Hill, 1966.
Theory of Literature (with Austin Warren). New York: Harcourt, 1949; 2nd rev. ed., A Harvest Book, 1956; 3rd rev. ed., 1962.

2. Articles (listed chronologically)

"The Pearl: An Interpretation of the Middle English Poem." *Studies in English by Members of the English Seminar of Charles University*, 4. Prague: 1933, pp. 1–33. Reprinted (with some corrections) in *Sir Gawain and the Pearl: Critical Essays*, ed. Robert J. Blanch. Bloomington: Indiana University Press, 1966, pp. 3–36.
"The Theory of Literary History." *Travaux du Cercle Linguistic de Prague*, 6. Prague: Charles University, 1936, pp. 179–91. Revised in "Literary History." *Literary Scholarship: Its Aims and Methods*, ed. Norman Foerster. Chapel Hill: University of North Carolina Press, 1941, pp. 91–103, 226–29, 239–55.
"Literary Criticism and Philosophy." *Scrutiny* 5 (1937): 375–83. Reprinted in *The Importance of Scrutiny*, ed. Eric Bentley. New York: G. Stewart, 1948, pp. 23–30.
"Van Wyck Brooks and a National Literature." *American Prefaces* 7 (1942): 292–306.
"The Revolt against Positivism in Recent European Literary Scholarship." *Twentieth Century English*, ed. W. S. Knickerbocker. New York: Philosophical Library, 1946, pp. 67–89. Reprinted in *Concepts of Criticism*, pp. 256–81.
"Czech Literature" and "Slovak Literature" and forty articles on major Czech literary figures since 1870. *Columbia Dictionary of Modern European Literatures*, ed. Horatio Smith. New York: Columbia University Press, 1947, pp. 185–91, 757–59, etc.
"Six Types of Literary History." *English Institute Essays 1946*. New York: Columbia University Press, 1947, pp. 107–26.
"Introduction" to Nikolay Gogol, *Dead Souls*. New York: Rinehart, 1948, pp. v–xi.
"Coleridge: Philosophy and Criticism." *The English Romantic Poets: A Review of Research*, ed. T. M. Raysor. New York: Modern Language Association, 1950, pp. 95–117; rev. ed., 1956, pp. 110–37; 3rd rev. ed., ed. Frank Jordan, 1972, pp. 209–31.
"Benedetto Croce, Literary Critic and Historian." *Comparative Literature* 5 (1953): 75–82.
"The Criticism of T. S. Eliot." *Sewanee Review* 64 (1956): 398–443.
"Masterpieces of Realism and Naturalism." *World Masterpieces*, ed. Maynard Mack, 2. New York: W. W. Norton, 1956; 2nd rev. ed., 1964; 3rd rev. ed., 1973; 4th rev. ed., 1979.
"Literary Theory, Criticism, and History." *Sewanee Review* 68 (1960): 1–19.
"Style in Literature, Closing Statement." *Style In Language*, ed. Thomas

A. Sebeok. Cambridge, Massachusetts: Technology Press and John Wiley, 1960, pp. 408–19.

"Introduction: A Brief History of Dostoevsky Criticism." *Dostoevsky, A Collection of Critical Essays,* ed. René Wellek. Englewood Cliffs, New Jersey: Prentice-Hall, 1962, pp. 1–15.

"Some Principles of Criticism." *Times Literary Supplement,* July 26, 1963, p. 49. Reprinted in *The Critical Moment: Essays on the Nature of Literature.* London: Faber and Faber, 1964, pp. 40–47; also New York: McGraw Hill, 1964.

"The Literary Criticism of Frank Raymond Leavis." *Literary Views: Critical and Historical Essays,* ed. Carroll Camden. Chicago: University of Chicago Press, 1964, pp. 175–99.

"Irving Babbit, Paul More, and Transcendentalism." *Transcendentalism and Its Legacy,* ed. Myron Simon and Thornton H. Parsons. Ann Arbor: University of Michigan Press, 1966, pp. 185–203.

"French 'Classicist' Criticism in the Twentieth Century." *The Classical Line: Essays in Honor of Henri Peyre, Yale French Studies* 38 (1967): 47–71.

"On Rereading I. A. Richards." *Southern Review* 3 (1967): 533–54.

"Why Read E. T. A. Hoffman?" *Midway* 8 (1967): 49–56.

"The Literary Criticism of Friedrich Gundolf." *Contemporary Literature* 9 (1968): 394–405.

"Czech Literature: East or West?" *Czechoslovakia: Past and Present,* ed. Miloslav Rechcígl, Jr., 2. The Hague: Mouton, 1969, pp. 893–902.

"Literary Criticism." *Encyclopedia of World Literature in the Twentieth Century,* 2, ed. W. B. Fleischmann. New York: Ungar, 1969, pp. 284–328.

"The Supposed Influence of Vico on England and Scotland in the Eighteenth Century." *Giambattista Vico: An International Symposium,* ed. Giorgio Tagliacozzo and Hayden V. White. Baltimore: The Johns Hopkins University Press, 1969, pp. 215–23.

"Comparative Literature at Yale." *Ventures: Magazine of the Yale Graduate School* 10 (1970): 24–32.

"American Criticism of the Last Ten Years." *Yearbook of Comparative and General Literature,* 20. Bloomington: University of Indiana Press, 1971, pp. 5–14.

"Šalda, František Xaver." *Encyclopedia of World Literature in the Twentieth Century,* 3, ed. W. B. Fleischmann. New York: Ungar, 1971, pp. 222–23.

"The Early Literary Criticism of Walter Benjamin." *Rice University Studies: Studies in German in Memory of Robert L. Kohn* 57 (1971): 123–34.

"Kenneth Burke and Literary Criticism." *Sewanee Review* 79 (1971): 171–88.

"R. P. Blackmur Re-examined." *Southern Review* N.S. 7 (1971): 825–45.

"Russian Formalism." *Arcadia Zeitschrift für vergleichende Literaturwis-senschaft* 6 (1971): 175–86.

"Albert Thibaudet." *Modern French Criticism from Proust and Valéry to Structuralism,* ed. J. K. Simon. Chicago: University of Chicago Press, 1972, pp. 85–107.

"The Attack on Literature," *American Scholar* 42 (1972): 27–42.

"Baroque in Literature," 1, 188–95; "Classicism in Literature," 1, 449–56; "Literary Criticism," 1, 596–607; "Evolution in Literature," 2, 169–74; "Literature and Its Cognates," 3, 81–89; "Periodization in Literary History," 3, 481–86; "Realism in Literature," 4, 51–56; "Romanticism in Literature," 4, 187–98; "Symbol and Symbolism in Literature," 4, 337–45—all in *Dictionary of the History of Ideas,* ed. Philip P. Wiener. New York: Scribner's, 1973.

"The Fall of Literary History." *Geschichte: Ereignis und Erzählung,* ed. Reinhart Kosseleck and Wolf-Dieter Stempel. Munich: Wilhelm Fink Verlag, 1973, pp. 427–40.

"John Crowe Ransom's Theory of Poetry." *Literary Theory and Structure: Essays in Honor of William K. Wimsatt,* ed. Frank Brady, John Palmer, and Martin Price. New Haven: Yale University Press, 1973 [actually 1972], pp. 179–98.

"Poulet, Du Bos, and Identification." *Comparative Literature Studies* 10 (1973): 173–93.

"Walter Benjamin's Literary Criticism in His Marxist Phase." *The Personality of the Critic (Yearbook of Comparative Literature),* 2, ed. Joseph P. Strelka. University Park and London: Pennsylvania State University Press, 1973, pp. 168–78.

"Cleanth Brooks, Critic of Critics." *Sewanee Review* 10 (1974): 125–52.

"Introduction" to Thomas G. Masaryk, *The Meaning of Czech History,* trans. Peter Kussi. Chapel Hill: University of North Carolina Press, 1974, pp. vii–xxiii.

"Poetics, Interpretation, and Criticism." *Modern Language Review* 69 (1974): xxi–xxxi.

"A. C. Bradley, Shakespeare and the Infinite." *From Chaucer to Giblon: Essays in Memory of Curt A. Zimansky.* Iowa City: University of Iowa Press, 1975, pp. 85–103.

"Criticism as Evaluation." *Proceedings of the American Philosophical Society* 119 (1975): 397–400.

"Max Kommerell as Critic of Literature." *Teilnahme und Spiegelung: Festschrift für Horst Rudiger,* ed. Bela Allemann and Erwin Koppen. Berlin: Walter de Gruyter, 1975, pp. 485–98.

"Yvor Winters Rehearsed and Reconsidered." *Denver Quarterly* 10 (1975): 1–27.

"Collaborating with Austin Warren on *Theory of Literature.*" *Teacher and Critic: Essays by and about Austin Warren,* ed. Myron Simon and Harvey Gross. Los Angeles: The Plantin Press, 1976, pp. 68–75.

"Ezra Pound's Literary Criticism." *Denver Quarterly* 11 (1976): 1–20.

"The Price of Progress in Eighteenth-Century Reflections on Literature." *Transactions of the Fourth International Congress on the Enlightenment,* 5 *(Studies on Voltaire and the Eighteenth Century,* ed. T. Bestermann, 155). Oxford: The Voltaire Foundation and the Taylor Institution, 1976, pp. 2265–84.

"Vilém Mathesius (1882–1945), Founder of the Prague Linguistic Circle." *Sound, Sign and Meaning: Quinquagenary of the Prague Linguistic Circle,* ed. Ladislav Matějka. Ann Arbor: University of Michigan Press, 1976, pp. 6–14.

"Foreword" to Jan Mukařovský, *The Word and Verbal Art: Selected Essays,* trans. and ed. John Burbank and Peter Steiner. New Haven: Yale University Press, 1977, pp. x–xiii.

"The Literary Theory of William K. Wimsatt." *Yale Review* 66 (1977): 178–92.

"Reflections on My *History of Modern Criticism.*" *PTL: A Journal of Descriptive Poetics and Theory of Literature* 2 (1977): 417–27.

"Virginia Woolf as Critic." *Southern Review* 13 (1977): 419–37.

"Edmund Wilson (1895–1972)." *Comparative Literature Studies* 15 (1978): 97–123.

"The Literary Criticism of Ernst Robert Curtius." *PTL: A Journal of Descriptive Poetics and Theory of Literature* 3 (1978): 25–43.

"The New Criticism: Pro and Contra." *Critical Inquiry* 4 (1978): 611–24.

"Allen Tate: Literary Theorist and Critic." *Englische und amerikanische Literaturtheorie,* 2, ed. R. Ahrens and E. Wolff. Heidelberg: Carl Winter, 1979, pp. 557–72.

"Prospect and Retrospect." *Yale Review* 69 (1980): 301–12.

SECONDARY SOURCES

No attempt is made to list all works referred to in the Notes and References. Excluded are the large number of newspaper articles on Wellek and the many reviews of his books.

AUERBACH, ERICH. "*A History of Modern Criticism: 1750–1950.*" *Romanische Forschungen* 67 (1955): 387–97. This relativistic discourse (in German) clarifies the encyclopedic perspectivism of Volumes 1 and 2 but rejects Wellek's assumption that criticism is a unified subject.

BORKLUND, ELMER. "René Wellek." *Contemporary Critics.* London: St. James Press/New York: St. Martin's Press, 1977, pp. 507–12. English survey attacks Wellek's theorizing.

BUCCO, MARTIN. "Profile of a Contemporary: René Wellek." *Wordsworth Circle* 9 (1978): 269–74. Describes Wellek's contribution to Romanticism scholarship.

————. "René Wellek: Profession of Criticism." *Journal of Comparative Literature and Aesthetics* 1 (Winter 1978): 13–24. An account of Wellek's formative years and achievement.

CESERANI, REMO. "Ritratti critici di contemporanei." *Belfagor* 24 (1969): 547–78. Analyzes Wellek's work, with particular reference to Czech sources and Italian reputation.

DEMETZ, PETER. Introduction. *Essays on Czech Literature*. By René Wellek. The Hague: Mouton, 1963, pp. 7–10. Describes Wellek's major contributions to Czech studies.

HOLTHUSEN, H. E. "System und Geschichte der kritischen Intelligenz: René Welleks Beitrage zur Literaturwissenschaft." *Kritisches Verstehen*. Munich: Piper, 1961, pp. 197–215. Appraises the originality and learning in *History of Criticism*.

MOLIN, SVEN ERIC. "Criticism in Vacuo." *University of Kansas City Review* 24 (1957): 156–60. Wellek's *History* moves from critic to critic rather than from criticism to poetry.

NELSON, LOWRY, JR. "René Wellek." *Encyclopedia of World Literature in the Twentieth Century*, 4, ed. W. B. Fleischmann. New York: Ungar, 1975, pp. 391–93. Considers Wellek's critical position and significance in world literature.

NICHOLS, STEPHEN G. JR. Introduction. *Concepts of Criticism*. By René Wellek. New Haven and London: Yale University Press, 1963, pp. ix–xv. Discusses Wellek's struggle to clarify methodological issues.

SCAGLIONE, ALDO. "*Theory of Literature*." *Romance Philology* 11 (1958): 400–08. Reception of *Theory* in America and Europe. Lists dozens of reviews in American, British, Italian, German, and Spanish periodicals.

SUTTON, WALTER. "Histories, Theories, and Critiques of Criticism." *Modern American Criticism*. Englewood Cliffs, New Jersey: Prentice-Hall, 1963, pp. 229–37. Poses questions raised by *Theory of Literature*.

UITTI, KARL D. "The Study of Language and Literature." *Linguistics and Literary Theory*. New York: W. W. Norton, 1969, pp. 169–93. Summarizes Wellek's aesthetic linguistic consciousness in *Theory of Literature*.

WEBSTER, GRANT. *The Republic of Letters: A History of Postwar American Literary Opinion*. Baltimore and London: The Johns Hopkins University Press, 1979, pp. 177–89. Thomas S. Kuhn's *The Structure of Scientific Revolutions* is the model for Webster's classification of Wellek as "Theorist of the Aesthetic" under the constricted paradigm or charter "Tory Formalism."

WINNER, THOMAS G., and JOHN P. KASIK. "René Wellek's Contribution to American Literary Scholarship." *Forum* 2 (1977): 21–31. Describes Wellek's integration of Slavic, English, and American literary thought.

Index

182   RENÉ WELLEK

Sartre, Jean Paul, 131, 153
Saussure, Ferdinand de, 64
Sayce, R. A., 86
Scaglione, Aldo, 54, 55, 80, 156
Scalvini, Giovita, 116, 119
Schelling, F. W. J., 35, 51, 74, 85, 102,
    103, 106, 113, 114, 119, 142
Scherer, Edmond, 134
Scherer, William, 144
Schiller, Friedrich, 52, 82, 93, 100, 101,
    102, 106, 109, 114, 127, 128, 145, 146
Schlegel, August Wilhelm, 32, 74, 92,
    98, 100, 101, 102, 103, 104, 106, 109,
    113, 124, 125, 126, 139
Schlegel, Friedrich, 32, 74, 91, 98, 101,
    102, 103, 104, 106, 109, 113, 126
Schlegel, Johann Elias, 97
Schleiermacher, Friedrich, 113, 146
Schmidt, Erich, 144
Scholarship, literary, 20, 24, 30, 36, 37,
    40–41, 44–50, 53, 58–59, 71, 77, 92,
    99, 144, 153, 156, 157–58
Scholes, Robert, 88
Schopenhauer, Arthur, 19, 36, 101, 114,
    128, 146, 147
Schorer, Mark, 95, 106, 157
Schubarth, Carl Ernst, 126
Scott, Sir Walter, 40, 74, 105, 120, 130,
    138, 139
Sensibility, 67, 107, 119
Settembrini, Luigi, 119
Setting, 59, 107
Shakespeare, William, 19, 20, 40, 47, 56,
    58, 59, 94, 98, 99, 103, 106, 109, 113,
    122, 124, 125, 126, 127, 128, 138, 139,
    143, 145, 148, 149
Shapiro, Karl, 76
Shaw, George Bernard, 38, 130, 151
Shaw, Priscilla W., 29
Shelley, Percy Bysshe, 20, 36, 38, 74,
    105, 108, 120, 122, 124, 137, 138, 148
Shine, Hill, 52
Shipley, Joseph T., 43
Shklovsky, Viktor, 22, 39
Sidney, Sir Philip, 45
Sign, 42, 43, 64
Simmons, Ernest J., 50
Simmons, Robert W., 144

Sincerity, 60, 106, 118, 120, 123, 124,
    125, 133, 143
Sismondi, Charles Léonard Simonde de,
    117
Sitwell, Osbert, 38
Skelton, John, 86
Sládek, J. V., 20
Slavic literature and criticism, 27, 39–42,
    50–51, 58, 70–73, 75, 154
Smetana, Bedřich, 18
Smith, James C., 68
Society and literature, 41, 44, 60–61, 73,
    85, 105, ,117, 122, 123, 128, 129, 130,
    141–42, 152
Solger, F. W., 113
Solger, Karl Wilhelm Ferdinand, 91
Sophocles, 91, 98
Sources, 72, 144, 149
Southey, Robert, 36, 105
Spears, Monroe K., 157–58
Spencer, Benjamin T., 79
Spencer, Terence, 59
Spenser, Edmund, 20, 37, 47, 96, 106
Spielhagen, Friedrich, 145
Spiller, Robert E., 68
Spingarn, Joel E., 153, 155
Spitzer, Leo, 66, 76, 79, 83, 84, 85, 153
Staël, Mme. de (Ann-Louise Germaine,
    Baroness), 101, 108, 109, 111, 126
Staiger, Emil, 77
Standards. See Norms, Evaluation
Stauffer, Donald, 54, 55
Steiner, George, 88
Steiner, Peter, 72
Stendhal (Henri Beyle), 101, 109, 110,
    131, 133, 146
Stephen, Leslie, 138
Sterne, Laurence, 99, 126, 145
Stevens, Wallace, 82
Stewart, Dugald, 34
Stilforscher, 66, 75, 83
Strachey, Lytton, 38, 153
Strakhov, Nikolay, 143
Stříbny, Z., 71
Strindberg, August, 82
Structure, 26, 42, 62–63, 64, 67, 68,
    75–76, 88, 141, 146
Style and stylistics, 20, 24, 26, 33, 58,